Positive Personnel Practices

John E. Baird, Jr.
David J. Rittof

Quality Circles
Facilitator's Manual

Waveland Press, Inc.
Prospect Heights, Illinois

For information about this book, write or call:
    Waveland Press, Inc.
    P.O. Box 400
    Prospect Heights, IL 60070
    (312) 634-0081

ISBN 0-88133-010-8

Printed in the United States of America.

Contents

Preface

Today, more than ever before, the old saying that "we live in a changing world" is true. In American organizations, these changes can be seen most clearly in three areas:

a. Worker values. The "me generation" has grown up, and their value system now permeates almost every organization. Workers have a set of expectations concerning how they are to be treated and what role they are to play in the organizations that employ them, and when their expectations are not met they become disenchanted and nonproductive. At the same time, however, today's workforce is the most educated workforce ever to exist in this country, so that the contribution employees potentially can make to their employers is greater than ever before.

b. Economic realities. Hard economic times have caused organizations of all types to pay more attention to their costs, incomes, and worker productivity. The need to compete effectively with other nations who already have achieved high productivity levels has made many organizations even more eager to increase their workers' effectiveness. But for most organizations, the ability to maximize productivity while minimizing costs has literally become a matter of survival.

c. Management theories. Increasingly, scholars writing about the "best" ways to manage people are emphasizing worker participation in organizational decision-making. The new Theory Z, which has formalized the approach to management taken by the Japanese during the past 25 years, stresses trust between workers and management, and suggests that the development of that trust can come about only when labor and management participate together in organizational decision-making and problem-solving. In turn, this trust has been shown to bring about increased productivity, increased worker morale, reduced turnover and absenteeism, improved quality of work, and enhanced organizational success.

It should be clear, then, that all three changes are moving in the same direction. Today's worker has both the desire and the ability to participate in organizational decision-making. Today's economic climate makes it necessary for management to involve employees in decision-making in order to maximize productivity. Today's management theorist, perhaps reflecting these realities, calls upon management to institute programs which involve employees in work-related decisions. And all of these things ultimately have led to the system which is presented by this manual and the two which go with it: Quality Circles.

Briefly, Quality Circles are groups of people from the same work area who meet together on a regular basis to identify, analyze, and solve quality and other problems in their area. As such, then, Quality Circles are not mysterious, magic, or even new. They are simply common sense. Quality Circles are a management system or tool whereby participative decision-making can be implemented and maintained throughout the organization to achieve the involvement and productivity discussed above. However, while they are simple in concept, implementing them is not so simple. And that leads us to the purpose of this manual: to describe how the Facilitator of Quality Circles should implement and then maintain and expand the Quality Circles system in his or her own organization.

Implementing Quality Circles requires two types of activities. The first is structuring and gaining support for the system; the second is training the participants. The **Quality Circles Participant's Manual** and the **Quality Circles Leader's Manual** which accompany this book deal primarily with the training activities, presenting the information which circle leaders and circle participants will need to know in order to participate effectively in Quality Circle activities. The purpose of this book, then, is to describe how the system should be structured and implemented, and to discuss some ways in which circle leaders and participants should be taught the skills they need.

You will find this book helpful both in preparing to lead the Quality Circles process, and in developing your skills as a leader in your organization. But above all, by using the ideas and principles discussed in this book, you will be able to make a significant, quantifiable contribution to your organization — a contribution which helps the organization to adjust to today's changing worker, economy, and management philosophy.

1

An Overview to
Implementing Quality Circles

To initiate an effective Quality Circles system in an organization requires a great deal of planning, thought, and work. While most employees will be eager to participate (and most managers will say they are eager to start them), the actual implementation of Quality Circles is not something that is easily or quickly done. The program facilitator must devote a great deal of time to the program, at least initially; however, the success of the program is directly related to the time initially spent, so that it is time well invested.

In this chapter, we will consider some specific things that need to happen if Quality Circles are to be implemented successfully. We will first discuss the concept in general, gaining an acquaintance with the approach and philosophy embodied in Quality Circles. Then we will outline the sequence of events which must occur if the program is to be successful. All of this should help you to determine what you need to do to implement Quality Circles successfully in your own organization.

Introduction to Quality Circles

Today's organization continues to experience difficulties in poor quality work, employee apathy, low morale, high turnover and absenteeism, and low productivity. While a great deal of time, money, and effort have been devoted to the improvement of these things, only recently has there emerged a single, relatively comprehensive approach to dealing with these problems simultaneously. That approach is Quality Circles. Repeatedly, Quality Circles have proven an effective means of drawing upon the previously untapped potential hidden in an organization's work force. Today's worker is educated, imaginative, creative, motivated, and more than anyone else, acquainted with the problems he or she encounters daily in his or her job. Quality Circles simply create an opportunity for these people to use their knowledge and skills to deal with the problems they face, and to provide organizational

1

support for their doing so. In this manner, then, Quality Circles help management to draw upon their human resources as they work to make their organization as efficient and productive as possible.

An enormous body of research exists demonstrating that workers who have no input to the decisions that affect them ultimately lose interest in the well-being of their organization. They simply cease to care, and instead look toward other sources of satisfaction: more money, more benefits, better working conditions, and so on. Workers who are involved in decision-making, however, usually care very much about the success of their organization. They work with management to identify and solve problems, and to develop more efficient work flow. They identify more with their organization, and they derive satisfaction from the work itself. Above all, they realize that management holds them in some esteem and is anxious to listen to and use their ideas, and as a result they come to trust management more and to value themselves as human beings more. The participative style of management brought about by Quality Circles therefore helps people to take pride in their work, their organization, and ultimately, themselves.

While employees usually are anxious to participate in Quality Circles programs, there are some conditions, however, which must exist in an organization before Quality Circles can be of maximum benefit. These conditions include:

1. Some value placed on innovation. Managers who feel "we've always done it this way, so it must be the right way" will not be receptive to Quality Circles action plans and suggestions, and a Quality Circle in their area probably would not be very successful. Creative, improvement-oriented change must be valued to some degree by management before Quality Circles can be of benefit.

2. Some expertise among employees and supervisors. If everyone in the organization is new, or if workers and supervisors do not know their own jobs very well, then asking them to participate in Quality Circles probably would be unproductive. People should have had a chance to get to know their job-related problems reasonably well before they are asked to participate, and they should have some knowledge of how their problems might be solved.

3. Reasonable clarity in organizational structure. People must have some idea of who reports to whom in the organization; otherwise, the Quality Circle system will be difficult and confusing to administer, and the circle members are likely to become frustrated at management's inability to respond to them.

4. General employee satisfaction with compensation. While no one believes he or she is paid enough, employees must be reasonably satisfied with their compensation before they are asked to participate in Quality Circles. If the work force strongly believes that they are not paid fairly by management, for example, they will not be enthusiastic when management comes to them and asks them to develop long-range solutions to their work-related problems.

5. General employee satisfaction with supervision. Since the immediate supervisor typically leads the Quality Circle meetings, employee participants must have generally good feelings toward that individual. Typically, if the meetings are conducted by a supervisor who is strongly disliked by his or her people, the group will not be very enthusiastic in carrying out their activities.

6. Reasonable levels of job security. Employees who fear for their jobs, either due to impending layoffs, reductions in force, potential firings, or the closing of the facility in which they work, generally will be too preoccupied with these concerns and unable to concentrate on the tasks facing the group.

7. A desire to participate. Not every employee will find Quality Circles appealing. Some simply want to do their jobs, and then go home. For that reason, participation in Quality Circles usually is on a voluntary basis; you do not want to force people to participate if they have no desire to do so.

8. Some value placed on people. A few managers believe that "employees should be seen and not heard." They are autocratic in their management because they believe employees have nothing to offer. They tell employees what to do and how to do it, because they believe employees need to be told and cannot think for themselves. Such managers are unlikely to find Quality Circles a worthwhile investment of their employees' time, nor are they likely to listen to the ideas coming out of a Quality Circle group. After all, they know all the answers already. Quality Circles should not be started in areas or organizations headed by such managers. A reasonable attempt may be made to change this person's attitude toward people, but if that attempt fails, the manager should be left out of the process (or the organization should seek some other means of involving employees and improving productivity).

Probably none of these conditions is "hard and fast." In fact, Quality Circles occasionally have served to correct some of the situations described above. For the most part, however, the chances for success of a Quality Circles program are much improved if those circles are started in organizations and departments or units which meet the criteria outlined above.

Steps in Implementing Quality Circles

No two organizations implement Quality Circles in exactly the same way. In fact, one of the biggest mistakes you could make would be to take another organization's Quality Circles system and try to transplant it directly to your own. It probably will not work. Every organization is unique, and therefore every organization must go through a relatively unique process to implement its Quality Circles system. However, there are some basic stages through which you probably will go, and these stages are outlined below.

A. Discovering Quality Circles

The first step is for someone in the organization to discover the Quality Circles concept. Upon hearing of it, that person may search for literature that will provide additional information, and may also talk to other people about the idea. Information is shared; seminars sometimes are attended; perhaps the International Association of Quality Circles (IAQC) is contacted. Gradually, people in the organization come to know about Quality Circles.

B. Developing Initial Support

At some point, someone in the organization having a reasonably high level of authority must endorse the idea. Often, this person is the one who "discovered" the concept in the first place. Just as often, however, this person is told of Quality Circles by a subordinate, finds the concept interesting, and asks for more information. Eventually, this person may decide that "we should do that here." He or she may talk to other managerial personnel, and they may also support the idea. Eventually, these people provide the initial support for the program.

C. Setting Preliminary Objectives

Early in the process, the support group must define what the objectives of the Quality Circle program will be. This objective could be stated as simply as: "Enhance the quality of the product, service, and working life." On the other hand, it could be stated in considerably more detail:

1. Reduce errors and enhance quality
2. Inspire more effective teamwork
3. Provide job involvement

    4. Increase employee motivation
    5. Create problem solving capabilities
    6. Build an attitude of "Problem Prevention"
    7. Improve company communications
    8. Develop harmonious manager/worker relationships
    9. Promote personal and leadership development
  10. Develop a greater safety awareness

This could be expanded even further:

  11. Develop cost consciousness
  12. Promote greater productivity without speedup
  13. Build increased energy awareness and conservation
  14. Improve employee morale
  15. Develop a reputation for quality so as to be competitive and im-
      prove job security
  16. Provide for personal growth through training
  17. Provide opportunities for recognition

Naturally, the list they develop does not have to include all of the items listed above. What is important is that the support group has an opportunity to participate in selecting those objectives that are important to them. There are many reasons why people at all levels in an organization may support Quality Circles. In developing this preliminary list of objectives, the group should try to include items which later may better assure others' enthusiasm and support.

D. Building Management Support

This is a crucial step that must occur if the Quality Circle program is to be successfully initiated and maintained.

There are three main factors in developing management support:

    1. *Level in the organization.* Strive for support at the highest level in the organization. This may be a Vice President, President, or even the Chairman of the Board. It is best to have the blessing of the chief executive officer if possible. Managers at lower levels have often ex-pressed the concern: "I support the concept wholeheartedly, but I am reluctant to stick my neck out until I find out whether it has sup-port at a higher level. I have been burned too many times in the past." This concern is set to rest when someone at a high level is openly supportive.

    2. *Management support in the organizations that have Circle mem-bers.* The areas in which Quality Circles are to be started must be headed by managers supportive of the process.

3. *Depth of management support.* As many people in the management structure as possible should be supporters of the program.
There are a number of ways to go about building depth of management support. One is to talk about the program. Use every opportunity to express enthusiasm for this concept of worker participation.
At times this may seem a discouraging process, as your words appear
to fall upon deaf ears. However, many people need time to ponder
such innovative concepts. Talk to these people on a continuing basis. Provide them with literature that you feel would be useful. The
response time will vary: some will become as enthusiastic as you are
on the first contact. Others will take longer.

E. Deciding to Start

Finally, the decision to start will be made. Again, this should occur at the
highest level possible. It should not be, "OK, we will let you do it." Rather, it
must be, "We are ready to move ahead and will provide the kind of support
necessary to make it an organizational commitment."

F. Engaging a Consultant

Before proceeding further, the organization probably should select a consultant. This costs some money, but experience has shown that it is an investment which, in the long run, saves money and results in a better program.
The cost of a consultant may be between $700 and $900 a day. The consultant will be engaged for a minimum of one day and perhaps as much as a
week or more.

The consultant should be able to furnish a list of satisfied clients specifically
in the field of Quality Circles. He or she should be able to do much more than
simply make presentations to management, teach facilitators, and instruct
Circle leaders. He or she should have the necessary training materials and
aids. Further, he or she should be able to furnish Circle facilitators, leaders,
and members with training materials that they can use to study during the
training phase. Perhaps above all, he or she should have a broad enough
grasp of employee relations and personnel management to be able to structure a program which is consistent with your policies and practices, with your
organizational objectives, and with the law.

Finally, the consultant should work with you to assure that the resulting
Quality Circle program belongs to your organization. It should be *your*
program, not the consultant's.

G. Organizing the Steering Committee

The Steering Committee is the group that provides overall guidance and
direction for Quality Circle activities. The Steering Committee consists of

management level or staff personnel who have an interest in the Quality Circle activities. Committee members should represent various major functions of the organization, such as manufacturing, quality control, education and training, personnel, finance, engineering, and marketing. In many unionized organizations, union leadership is invited to participate on the Steering Committee.

The levels represented by Steering Committee members will vary from middle management to top level executive personnel. In many organizations, the chief executive officer is a member of the Steering Committee.

H. Selecting the Facilitator(s)

One of the key initial steps to be taken by the Steering Committee is the selection of the Facilitator(s). This person or group will have primary responsibility for implementing and coordinating the Quality Circles system.

I. Finalizing of the Objectives

The preliminary objectives have already been established, but these need to be finalized. By this time management will be far enough along in Circle activities to have much clearer ideas about what to select as final objectives.

J. Developing the Implementation Plan

The all-important implementation plan is prepared by the Steering Committee. This is really a combination of two or more documents. One document is the Quality Circle procedure which defines the way Quality Circles will interact with the other organizations. An important part of the procedure is the objectives which have already been established. The procedure also defines those items that should *not* be addressed by Quality Circles. The other document is the implementation time table, which denotes all of the activities that must occur and when they should happen.

The implementation plan is a vital document that takes time and care to develop. It should not be done by having the Steering Committee ask the facilitator to "put something together and we'll take a look at it." Rather, it should be done by various members of the Steering Committee talking to members of management at all levels. They should explain the Quality Circle concept and ask for suggestions on how it can best be implemented. They will get excellent suggestions that will help to customize the Quality Circle activities so that they fit best in the organization.

The consultant should guide the Steering Committee to assure an effective program and to enhance the likelihood of success. This also helps to avoid the development of variant plans that could result in disastrous consequences.

The involvement of all members of the Steering Committee is important. It should be their program. Their egos must be involved in guiding the program to a successful implementation.

K. Collecting Pre-implementation Data

Ultimately, someone will ask, "What kind of results are the Quality Circles producing?" To answer, it will be necessary to have "before and after" data. Before starting Quality Circles, base line information should be gathered for future reference. This information should be in the areas of quality, cost, absenteeism, turnover, attitudes, safety performance, schedule adherence, cost of rework, scrap, labor costs per unit of product, or volume of units produced, depending upon the objectives formulated by the Steering Committee at Step I.

After Quality Circles have been in operation for some time, additional data can be gathered and compared to the baseline measurements. This will provide evidence to convince management and to serve as a valuable feedback to Circle members who are also highly interested in what they are accomplishing.

While certain kinds of baseline data can be determined at some later time by examining on-going records, occasionally it must be collected ahead of time or it cannot be collected at all. One example is employee attitude surveys. There is no way that employees can "remember" how they felt about their organization, their job, their supervision, or communications before the Quality Circle program started, if they are asked to do so several weeks later.

L. Conducting Briefings for Management and Union

There may be a number of people in management who have not been directly involved in Quality Circle activities up to this time. It may be advisable to inform these individuals now about what is occurring and the plans for the future. They may need to assist circle activities later, or they may wish to initiate Quality Circles in their own organizations at a later date. There will also be staff organizations who may have varying degrees of contact with the Quality Circles. Therefore, it is in the best interests of everyone that a full awareness of Quality Circles be established. There also may be a need to alleviate the fears of those who feel that Quality Circles represents some kind of threat to them. Everyone has to understand that they can help Quality Circles do a better job, and in turn, Quality Circles can help them do their job better.

Union officials also should be briefed about what is occurring so that they can respond to questions from their membership. It would be unfortunate to put union officers in the undesirable position of not understanding what was occurring among the people in their bargaining unit. The union officials, all the way from president to union stewards, are normally among the most responsive and receptive to this kind of activity. In fact, they often have been arguing for this kind of worker participation for years. Further, union stewards normally are members of the Quality Circles in their areas and are typically very enthusiastic.

M. Selecting Pilot Program Circle Leaders

Now comes the difficult task of determining which supervisors or managers will participate as leaders in the Quality Circle pilot program. The pilot program usually runs for five or six months and consists of just a few Circles. Who will these leaders be? By the time the word has circulated about the upcoming Quality Circle activities, often several supervisors have stepped forward and volunteered to be part of it. It may not be a case of recruiting who will be leaders of the pilot Circles; rather, it may be "How will we select from those that want to do it?"

The selection process is enhanced when the Steering Committee sets aside the time to interview candidates for Circle leaders positions. The conditions for success listed earlier in this chapter should also be considered when selecting Circle leaders. Finally, if departments having a great deal of work-related contact with one another are involved, a Circle probably should be started in each to promote coordination later on.

N. Developing Individual Leader Performance Goals

After the Circle leaders have been chosen, it is important that the Facilitator sit down with each and discuss performance criteria and goals. What is expected? What does each leader plan as far as his or her own activities are concerned? There will be questions in the minds of the leaders as to how much time will be utilized in the pursuit of these performance objectives and how well equipped they are to achieve them. Also, they will want to know what resources they can draw on to assure attainment. These performance goals must be acceptable to each leader. They must also be acceptable to the managers the leaders report to. Each performance goal should be written in such a way that it is measureable. Provision must be made for feedback so that both the leader and the manager will know how successfully each goal is being met.

O. Issuing Pre-publicity to Inform All Employees

There will be curiosity about what is going on. If the organization does not act to fill this gap, the grapevine will. The kind of publicity is important: you simply want to inform. If the publicity is too strong and too enticing, there will be a deluge of requests by employees to become involved in Quality Circles. Such requests management may not be prepared to handle. Information is all that is required at this time. Simply state that the organization is implementing Quality Circles on a pilot basis. After a pre-established number of months, the pilot activities will be completed and gradual expansion will occur. Make certain that employees understand that they are not being excluded on a permanent basis; their turn will come as soon as conditions permit.

The publicity can be issued in one of several ways:

- Letters to the employees' homes
- Employee newsletter or magazine
- Large group meetings
- Numerous small group sessions
- One-on-one by supervisors
- Bulletin board announcements
- Pay envelope "stuffers"

P. Conducting Training Classes

Facilitator. Training classes for the Facilitator are usually conducted by the consultant at the organization's location. Occasionally, an organization elects to send the Facilitator to an outside training course.

Leader. The original set of leaders for the pilot program activities are normally trained immediately after the Facilitator is trained by the consultant. This is not necessary, but it is nearly always done. After all, the consultant is already there and might as well be utilized as fully as possible during the kickoff phase.

Typically, the leader training classes are attended in part or in full by other members of management who have an interest in Quality Circle activities. Sometimes these are members of the Steering Committee.

Q. Initiating Circles

The leader, freshly trained in Quality Circle techniques, finalizes the membership in his or her Circle. This, in itself, may be no easy task. Take, for instance, the supervisor who had thirty-seven people reporting to him. Thirty-two wanted to be members of the one Quality Circle he was going to operate during the pilot phase. He solved the problem by simply putting 32 names into a hat and drawing out 8 of them. Other times the selection can be done by seniority, job classification, or some other basis.

R. Member Training

Brief training classes are used to teach Circle participants basic communication and group decision-making skills. Then the first several weeks of meetings are devoted to training Circle members in the techniques of problem solving. Quality Circle members receive instructions from their Circle leader.

The Facilitator is encouraged to attend these training sessions to provide backup for the leader as necessary. It is important that the leader carry the load, however. The Facilitator works behind the scenes, assisting the leader when necessary. There will be opportunities to apply some of the training techniques to actual problems during the training process.

S. Periodic Review by Steering Committee

Quality Circles is no different than any other kind of activity — it requires managing. It is vital that goals be established. It is also important that measurable milestones be put in place towards the achievement of these goals. That is the purpose of the implementation plan the Steering Committee establishes at an earlier phase. Now, we have moved ahead to a point where the progress must be checked against the plan.

The success the Steering Committee will have in performing this valuable function is contingent, in part, on the care with which the original implementation plan was drawn up. The milestones must be measureable or they cannot be evaluated with any degree of success. The results of the review by the Steering Committee should be conveyed to everyone who is directly affected.

This periodic review does something else: it provides information necessary to make modifications and corrections in Circle activities. Thus, it lays the foundation for the success of the entire program.

T. Expanding the program

Ultimately (typically in 6 months), the program may be expanded to new departments and groups. Managers who initially were non-committal about (or even opposed to) the program now may be enthusiastic about it, and eager to involve their own people. Employees who volunteered initially and were not chosen still may want to participate. Thus, using the lessons learned by the pilot project, the next stage is to expand the program to new areas, teaching new circle leaders and new circle participants the skills they will need, and then implementing the system in their areas.

U. Ending Group Involvement

Eventually, it will come time to phase one group out, perhaps replacing them with another. Perhaps the group has run out of ideas or problems; perhaps they have become interested in other things; or perhaps they simply have participated long enough and need to step aside to give others a chance. Whatever the situation, some recognition should be given this group for their efforts, and this recognition should be made public. Later in this book, we will consider some of the forms that such recognition might take.

Again, the actual sequence of steps you might implement in your own organization could differ somewhat from those outlined above. For example, an employee opinion survey might occur before any of these steps (rather than as a portion of collecting initial data), and might reveal the need for a Quality Circles system in the first place. Or a Facilitator might be chosen before the entire Steering Committee is in place. Nevertheless, the functions presented above must at some point in the process be completed in order for Quality Circles to have maximum effectiveness.

Summary

In this introductory chapter, we took a brief view of the nature of Quality Circles, the conditions which must exist to some degree if Quality Circles are to be effective, and the sequence of stages through which an organization should proceed when implementing a Quality Circles program. Having seen these things, we now are ready to consider in more detail each of the steps involved in this process.

2

Selling Quality Circles and Building Management Support

As we indicated repeatedly in the preceding chapter, the success of Quality Circles rests heavily upon the willingness of management to support the process. If top, middle, and lower-level managers view Quality Circles as something that will benefit the organization and ultimately benefit them as well, then their dedication to the process alone will virtually guarantee its success. On the other hand, if they are threatened by or hostile toward the system, then they will avoid it or, even worse, actively work to undermine it. One of your first tasks, then, is to "sell" the program to the management group, both by answering objections they might have and by promoting the very real advantages which Quality Circles can offer.

In this chapter, we will consider two basic activities involved in selling Quality Circles internally. First, we will suggest some commonly-heard objections to the program, and offer some potential responses. Then we will consider some techniques which can be used to build support at each level of management in the organization. By using this information in your own organization when necessary, you will do much to speed the acceptance of a Quality Circles program and to ensure its ultimate success.

Overcoming Objections

Those who are committed to Quality Circles probably did not need much convincing to see the potential benefits of the process, both to individuals and to organizations as a whole. Those who believe in Quality Circles probably have a basic belief about human nature which allows for the integration of human needs and potential with the goals and policies of organizations. However, many people may find (much to their discomfort) that the views and opinions that they hold as basic truths may not be shared by others who

13

are in a position to influence plans and decisions. In fact, the principles underlying Quality Circles may even be foreign or hostile to them.

When first explaining Quality Circles to people in your own organization, instead of positive interest or acceptance you may find most responses to be in the form of resistance or negative criticism. After evaluating a number of negative responses, you will find most of them to originate from one or more pre-established opinions or misconceptions:

A. Misunderstanding of the Quality Circle Concept

It is important that anyone entering into involvement with Quality Circles fully understand that Quality Circles is a tool for management support as well as for employee development. Quality Circles is not intended to subvert management in any manner, nor is it intended to turn policy making over to line employees. Above all, Quality Circles is not a substitute for, but rather is an addition to the regular quality function.

B. Resistance to Change

Any type of change may bring about a disruption of normal processes and procedures, and as a result many people who are accustomed to a certain set of "normal" operations will tend to feel uncomfortable with change. To many organizations with pre-established routines and structures, Quality Circles may represent an unacceptble amount of change.

C. Adherence to Experience

Most organizations have evolved through the diligent efforts of certain people. Many such people have formulated opinions and rules as the result of their own experience. People often cling tenaciously to their own principles and ideas and feel threatened to have them challenged by something new or foreign.

D. Distrust of People-Oriented Programs

Some persons really do not believe that subordinates can be trusted to perform their function without being threatened, coerced or cajoled into doing so. Such opinions may be the result of experience, training, or the basic psychological character of the individual.

Out of these perceptions or predispositions come some common objections to Quality Circles that you may encounter. These objections are presented below, along with some potentially appropriate reactions or responses.

a. It would take too much time from production activities

Although Quality Circles does require some time to be spent in non-production activities, the amount of time spent will not be great enough to reduce productivity seriously. The potential productivity benefits from Quality Circle activities, on the other hand, will considerably outweigh the small amount of lost production time.

b. *It would cost too much to get started*

Start-up costs can be relatively high. However, one must understand that the potential cost savings offered by Quality Circles on the average is six times the actual cost of the program.

c. *The organization is too small for that sort of activity*

The structure and activity of Quality Circles appears to be oriented toward large organizations which have formal training and manpower development organizations within them. Careful examination of the history and function of Quality Circles will show that this is not necessarily true. Quality Circles is adaptable to all sizes of organizations. Smaller organizations benefit as much from Quality Circles as do large organizations. One or two active circles in a small organization may represent a large percentage of employee participation and a proportionately larger potential benefit.

d. *Quality is the job of the "Quality Department," not the concern of line employees*

Such a statement represents a basic misunderstanding of the Quality function. Quality is not the responsibility of any single department, it is the responsibility of all persons having an input to the product or service. The principle of quality input from all levels is fundamental to Quality Circles.

e. *Employees are not interested in that type of activity*

Many people believe that the only things employees are interested in are better pay, better benefits and better working conditions. To one with such beliefs, it may be inconceivable that employees could actively pursue goals which are consistent with those of the organization. A person holding those beliefs (and who cannot be convinced otherwise) should not be part of the initial program. In addition, since participation by employees is voluntary, those who are not interested need not participate.

f. *Employees would put Circle activities above their work*

This simply represents a misunderstanding of the entire idea of Quality Circles. All Circle activities are directed toward improving employees' performance in their jobs. Circle activities and employees' work are the same thing.

g. *Employees would only use Circles to find ways to make things easier on themselves*

This represents a very negative view of employee participation. Why should anyone object if employees find a way to make things easier and better? Perhaps the phrase, "work smarter, not harder" best represents the goal of Quality Circles.

h. Employees would use the Circles to make demands on the organization

This is another misunderstanding of Quality Circles. Quality Circles is not a form of collective bargaining or a vehicle for employee grievances. Any power that the Circles have comes from management support.

i. Quality Circle activities would be best left to managers and engineers

Managers and engineers have always been looked to for solutions to problems. However, these are usually very busy people who may not have time to solve all work related problems, nor do they necessarily understand the routine intricacies of the work environment. Properly functioning Quality Circles can be a tremendous support to management and staff personnel.

We may tend to consider those who support Quality Circles as being people-oriented, and those who oppose Quality Circles as being traditionally task-orientated, much like McGregor's "Theory X." Such "Good Guy," "Bad Guy" labels can obscure an objective evaluation of the acceptance or rejection of Quality Circles. Objections may be offered out of a sincere apprehension about one or more of the concepts of Quality Circles. If this fear is adequately alleviated the objector may willingly accept the idea. Some objections, however, may come from more adamant sources, and the person making the objections may not be willing or ready to accept the rather progressive idea of Quality Circles. A Quality Circle advocate should try to assess the sources of objections. It would be unfortunate to abandon efforts to establish a potentially successful Quality Circles program on the basis of reconcilable objections. On the other hand it would be disastrous to try to force Quality Circles into an organization or department which is not ready for it.

Building Management Support

Before examining specific techniques for gaining management support, we first need to answer the question, "Who is Management?" In most organizations, we are dealing with five groups. First is highest level executive management. The Chief Executive Officer, Chief Operating Officer, and others at or just below their level must support the program if it is to be begun, and if it later is to be expanded. Thus, this is the first level to which we must look for support. The second level is executive line management: the people in charge of major functions in the organization. Directors of Manufacturing, Engineering, or Quality Control in a manufacturing environment, or Directors of Nursing, Ancillary Services, and so on in a health care organization must support the program if it is to be effective in departments beneath them. Third, middle level management must also be involved in the program, lest they instead feel left out, threatened, or hostile toward it. Thus, their support is important. Management in support organizations who are not directly involved in the Quality Circles process should also be asked for their support, for the implementation of Circle recommendations ultimately may involve them. Finally, first-level supervision is a part of their management team, and their active support obviously is needed — particularly among those who head circle meetings. However, since so much of the Quality Circle process is geared toward involving first-line supervisors at the outset, we will consider only the first four management groups here.

Highest Executive Level

Surprisingly, this level typically is one of the least difficult to convince and most supportive of the Quality Circles process throughout the program. This seems to be the case for several reasons. First, the drive to implement Quality Circles typically begins with a commitment from one or more of them, so that a great deal of attention is devoted to convincing them to begin and to sustain the program. They receive a rather thorough indoctrination into the philosophy and concept of Quality Circles.

Further, their personal need for involvement is small. Most executives at that level have been exposed by now to a considerable amount of material about the need for and success of using participative styles of managing to get the best results. They don't feel threatened by the changes Quality Circles may bring about. They are many levels away from day by day operation of the workers and Circles. They recognize they have quality and productivity problems and are searching for methods to improve their organization's performance.

However, if there is a lack of support at that level, what can be done? First, keep the executives informed as to what is happening and the good that is being generated. Second, get them involved in going and making speeches, bragging about the Quality Circles' results. If the Facilitator writes a speech for an executive to give, that executive has to read about the results, wants to give a good impression to the audience, and ends up being sold, or at least interested.

Third, there are other methods of involving or informing the executives via publicity. In the early stages of a program, one should be cautious about using the small pilot circle programs in advertising to customers. However, once the program is mature and making a significant impact on operations, it is useful in promoting some public goodwill — and this is a way to involve the executives and get their lasting support. Several companies also have prepared in-house videotapes to show around the corporation and thus get executive level support.

Executive-Line Management

At this level it usually is possible to distinguish strong QC programs from weak QC programs, depending upon the support or lack of it given by these people. Here is the manager who can make it work, or keep it from working. One important strategy is to have this manager own the program. While it may be installed by the quality organization or the training organization or the human resources people, it ultimately must be owned, funded, staffed, developed and operated by the line function. This approach helps to ensure the program's success. For example, when budgets must be cut, if Quality Circles is saving the line organization money, the budget for facilitators is less likely to be cut by the line executive.

Middle Line Management

Middle line management support seems to be the biggest and most difficult obstacle to overcome. Why is this so? Here are a few of the key causes:

1. They are afraid of losing their decision making authority.
2. They believe Quality Circles is a waste of time.
3. They fail to see its rewards for them.
4. They have no direct on-going involvement.
5. They are not measured or evaluated on whether they have Quality Circles, or on the results of Quality Circles.
6. They do not fully understand the concept.
7. They do not use the problem solving techniques themselves.
8. It was not their idea to have Quality Circles in their organization.

There are other subsidiary reasons, but these seem to be the primary ones.

To resolve these problems, you should implement an integrated approach for middle line managers designed to enhance their involvement.

First of all, middle line managers need to be brought into the decision process about Quality Circles in the very beginning. After executive management has made a "go" decision, the middle line managers expected to have Quality Circles need to be invited to attend a training class, the outcome of which hopefully will be a thorough understanding of the concept and its benefits to them. Thus, they will be prepared to "volunteer" to have circles in their organization. During this training, they will experience being a part of a Quality Circle, be given the opportunity to make decisions about how it will operate in their organization, and be shown how circle's achievements can be measured and operate to improve their own ratings of performance. Further, they will be shown how they might apply the principles and use the problem solving techniques in their own meetings. In this way, they will come to appreciate the value of this concept and to understand the need of the circles for their support.

Second, while the circles proceed, these managers need to be kept informed constantly of the activities in which circles are engaged. They need to be asked for their own ideas and suggestions, and when one of their circles has developed an action plan, they need to have the opportunity to review that plan before it is presented to top management.

Finally, the performance appraisal conducted for these managers needs to take into account whether or not they have circles in operation, and to reward those managers whose circles have brought about measurable results. In this way, the success of the circles is tied directly to the manager's own success, and his or her support of the process is greatly enhanced.

Support Organizations Management

With this group of managers, while it is desirable to have their whole-hearted support, such support is not critical to a successful Quality Circle program. Some thoughts about actions a facilitator might take to get this support are:

1. Include them in an early orientation session.
2. Involve them in the planning of how the Quality Circle program will be structured. If you use an advisory committee, see that some of them are included in its membership.
3. For such organizations as Training, Management Development, Human Resources and Quality Assurance, all of whom have some jurisdiction in the field of Quality Circles, sit down and work out all of their feelings, negative and positive, so that none of them feels they are being encroached upon.
4. Distribute results to them and give their organizations credit where it is deserved.
5. Finally, try and interest them in starting up Quality Circles in their own organizations.

Summary

While the concept of Quality Circles may seem common sense to you —
and it is common sense — other members of the management group may not
feel quite the same way. They may find the concept threatening, potentially
dangerous to their own position in the organization, or inconsistent with the
objectives they have been striving toward themselves during their tenure in
the organization. As a result, they may oppose this program, despite the fact
that, ultimately, it would work to their advantage.

In this chapter, we have considered some of the techniques you might use
to enlist the support of the management team. Most of the objections we
listed derived from misimpressions people commonly hold about the Quality
Circles process — misimpressions which can be cleared up by providing some
more detailed information. However, some of them may derive from a manager's philosophy concerning management and the nature of people, and
those objections may not be answerable — at least not to the satisfaction of the
person offering them. That person probably should not be involved in the
Quality Circles system, at least initially, and he or she probably would not
want to be involved anyway. But above all, you should work to enlist the
support of everyone possible, at each level of the organization. Hopefully, the
techniques suggested in this chapter will enable you to do that.

3

Planning for Quality Circles

When management support has been obtained, the next key to success with Quality Circles is careful planning for the entire process. Most of this planning is done by the Steering Committee, whose responsibility it is to guide and oversee the entire program, and to review and implement circle action plans when they are developed and presented. In this chapter, then, we will study the Steering Committee itself, noting its purpose, membership, and operation. Then we will turn to the planning process, suggesting a simple technique whereby the entire Quality Circle program can be laid out piece by piece. Finally, we will consider some methods whereby the success of the Quality Circles system can be tracked — an important consideration which must be confronted before the process itself is initiated.

The Steering Committee

As we saw in Chapter I, the Steering Committee is the body of people responsible for overseeing the Quality Circles program. The purpose of this committee, simply put, is to establish and maintain adherence to the operating guidelines of the Quality Circle program throughout the organization. Specifically, they establish the objectives of the program, lay out policies to guide its operations, meet regularly with the Facilitator to keep abreast of current happenings, provide guidance and direction when needed, help the Facilitator to coordinate the activities of different departments or units in the organization, help the circle leaders and participants to obtain information or resources they need to conduct their activities, and ultimately, review (usually with other members of management) participant presentations and determine whether the recommended actions are to be taken. While this is a rather long list of activities, each of which is important, we will focus on a few of them as they pertain to the planning of the circles process.

Committee Membership

In view of the scope of concerns addressed by the Steering Committee, it should be obvious that the Committee should consist of representatives of each major function in the organization — certainly those functions in which Quality Circles are to be begun. Clearly, too, these people generally should be supportive of the QC concept, since they will have responsibility for running it.

Who is selected as Chairman of the Steering Committee is not particularly critical, except that it certainly should be a person who will encourage and support a free flow of ideas, rather than one who is so dominant that the other members feel intimidated into accepting only one person's thinking. Frequently, the Chairman is a key person in the organization who sincerely believes in Quality Circles as a viable technique applicable to any work environment.

It is not necessary that membership on the Committee be limited to top-level managers, and, in actual practice, many successful Quality Circle programs are directed by a Committee made up of representatives of all strata of the organization. The Steering Committee, after all, should be designed to do just that — steer — not to dominate the Quality Circle program.

Production, quality control, engineering, finance, marketing, office administration, personnel, industrial relations and the union are examples of the broad spectrum of interests which should be represented on the Committee. The inclusion of such varied interests will help eliminate the possibility that some elements of the organization will feel that Quality Circles is something that is being done to them rather than with them. It tends to foster widespread ownership of the program, and it also serves to spread the concept into areas other than production. There is, similarly, less likelihood of any element of the organization being unresponsive or antagonistic to the Circles.

Among management people, there is sometimes a great hesitancy to even consider non-management personnel, and especially the union, as members of the Steering Committee. In some cases there is a fear that such a move will only serve to provide an inroad into co-management of the organization. It is indeed tragic that such concerns should interfere with the implementation of Quality Circles. However, it is precisely those organizations in which trust and openness do not exist which can benefit most from Circle involvement. Moreover, in such a suspicious atmosphere, Quality Circles will probably not work well, if at all, unless management makes membership on the Steering Committee available to all elements of the organization.

Quality Circles is a management philosophy, designed to improve communications and work attitudes throughout any organization. Nowhere can management better display their whole-hearted support to this concept than in their treatment of the Steering Committee at the very outset of implementing Quality Circles. The Committee should be granted the responsibility and the authority to make decisions governing the operation of the Quality Circles program. They must be allowed the time and resources to meet on a regular basis and to attend Circle meetings and management presentations. A Quality Circle Steering Committee, functioning as described here, is an important step toward a successful Quality Circle program in any organization.

Committee Activities

Operational Policies

The Committee should write and publish an overall policy statement concerning the objectives of the Quality Circle effort. In arriving at such a statement, the Committee must reflect the organization management's primary goals or reasons for initiating Quality Circles. This seems elementary, yet it is common for middle management personnel and Circle members alike to question top management's motives. In the absence of such a statement, everybody is left to their own suspicions. This is not to say that a written policy statement will totally preclude such suspicions, but it will go a long way toward that end. Such a statement serves to provide continuity of purpose as well as a point of departure in the event of a change in management's emphasis.

The Steering Committee should also be chartered to esbablish the organization policies and procedures to guide the day-to-day operation of Quality Circles. The initiation of a management philosophy as far-reaching as Quality Circles is difficult at best, and can be a bitterly frustrating experience if it is not well planned and systematically executed. Without the assistance of a broad-based Steering Committee and a well thought-out set of operational policies, the person setting out to develop Quality Circles in his or her organization will be faced with a continuing series of crises.

Selecting the Facilitator

One of the earliest and most significant challenges faced by the Steering Committee is the selection of the Facilitator. As the Facilitator is undoubtedly the single most important element in the Quality Circle organization, all factors concerning this position should be well thought-out and clearly delineated from the outset. What qualifications should this person bring to the job? Should the position be posted and candidates interviewed or will this person be selected?

Perhaps the best way to arrive at some of the answers is to begin with a complete description of the duties and responsibilities attendant to the position.

Among the things the Facilitator does are to promote and sell the program to others, both inside and outside the organization. Moreover, the Facilitator must act as a teacher who can introduce the concept to the management team and provide them with an in-depth orientation to the implications of Quality Circles for them and the organization. He or she is responsible for teaching the circle leaders (perhaps with initial assistance by an outside consultant) the skills they need to function effectively, and for teaching circle participants the skills they will need. He or she must attend many of the initial circle meetings, helping the circle leader both to lead effectively and to teach specific problem-solving skills to the participants.

Still other requirements of the Facilitator's function are to make presentations to management at all levels concerning the overall status of the Quality Circle program, and to respond to requests from outside the organization for information (or even personal presentations) on the subject. In addition, he or she must coordinate the circle activities, making sure that all circles know what the others are doing. The Facilitator ties the circles to the rest of the organization: when a circle decides they would like to have help or information from someone in the organization, it is the Facilitator who contacts and invites that person. When a circle needs information, guidance, or resources, the Facilitator is the first to know, and he or she must guide that circle toward the appropriate source; the Steering Committee, someone in management, some department in the organization, and so on.

Finally when it comes time to evaluate and expand the program, it is the responsibility of the Facilitator to obtain all appropriate information needed to judge the program's success or progress, and to present that information to the Steering Committee. Then, if the decision for expansion is made, the Facilitator must begin the whole sequence over again: teaching, coaching, coordinating, reporting, and so on.

Obviously, the Facilitator must be able to commit a great deal of time to the Quality Circles system, particularly at the beginning. If, for example, six circles are to be started initially, the Facilitator will need to spend at least 8 hours training the circle leaders, and then another 4 hours training each group of 20-25 participants. Then, when the meetings begin, the Facilitator will need to spend 6 hours per week (assuming weekly, one-hour meetings for each circle) attending those meetings, plus another hour every two or three weeks meeting with the circle leaders as a group. He or she also will spend at least 2 hours a month meeting with the Steering Committee, keeping them informed of current events. Finally, when the process is up and running, the Facilitator will be on an "on-call" status, taking time when it is needed to coordinate, coach, report, etc.

The qualities that make a good Facilitator, then, seem to be these:

- Commitment to the Quality Circles concept and process
- Ability to devote the necessary time
- Understanding of the organization, both technically and politically
- Skill as a communicator, both in formal presentations and informal interactions
- Respect by the organization in general

This is the sort of person for whom the steering committee should look. Typically, it is best if this person holds a management position, preferably high in a major department or unit of the organization.

Identifying Circle Leaders

The Steering Committee policies should determine the method of Circle Leader selection as well. As we have seen, the Quality Circle leader should be the person immediately above (on the organizational chart) the employees who are to act as circle participants. This person may be a supervisor, a foreman, or a department head (if no supervisors fall between department head and employees). He or she is responsible for their Quality Circle activities as well. If he or she supervises a large department in which more than one circle is started, he or she probably should lead each of the circles. If time is not available for multiple circle leadership, then only one circle should be started; it usually is best not to have someone other than the supervisor step in and serve as leader.

As a rule, leaders are selected from among those who volunteer to participate after management has been oriented to the Quality Circles process. However, this procedure has both its good and bad sides. The good side is that the circles led by these people probably will be. effective, because the leader will make them effective. After all, these people must believe in and be comfortable with the concept, or they would not have volunteered in the first place. The bad side, however, is that these may not be the people who could benefit most from Quality Circles. If they already are predisposed toward participative management, they probably have already found ways to involve their people in problem-solving. On the other hand, the autocratic supervisor who has never asked his or her people for their input probably is the one whose department would improve most if Quality Circles were to begin there. Thus, the risk of failure is greater with these people, but so too is the extent of the success which they might achieve.

Generally, then, the Steering Committee may want to use a combination

strategy for selecting circle leaders. They may take a few volunteers, knowing that in those areas the program probably will be successful, and thus will
build some momentum which, later on, will promote expansion to riskier
areas. However, they may also want to "volunteer" some leaders themselves — people whose departments need considerable improvement, and
whose management style also needs changing. By training these people carefully and then overseeing their activities carefully (perhaps by having the
Facilitator attend virtually every meeting for some time, or even by having the
supervisor's immediate superior attend frequently), the Steering Committee
may be able to achieve some spectacular successes in previously weak areas
of the organization.

Quality Circle Operations

What resources will be available to the Circles? The Steering Committee
should determine the amount and kind of resources a Circle may use to verify
their conclusions, and the method by which they may obtain them.

The duration and frequency of Circle meetings, the size of the Circles, the
time of day they will meet and in which organizations Circles will be started
are but a few of the details which should be set out very clearly. To avoid con-
fusion and perhaps even discouragement in the day-to-day program
operation, the Steering Committee should address as many potential problems as they can visualize.

Some additional considerations may be such things as: how and when
inter-circle projects will be handled; how Circle solutions will be implemented
into the non-circle work environment; how non-cooperative managers
should be approached; how competition between Circles will be treated, encouraged or discouraged; the rate of growth of the Quality Circle program;
where Circles will be introduced and how it will be done; how Facilitators and
Leaders will be trained; the use and involvement of outside consultation and
training; the timing and method of measurement of Quality Circle effectiveness; the rate of compensation and method of recording time spent on circle
activities, and, of course, how Quality Circle activities will be publicized.

What Circles Can Work On

One of the frequently overlooked, and thus most troublesome, details of
Quality Circle planning is the matter of what subjects Circles will be allowed to
explore. In most cases, it is a far simpler matter to state as explicitly as possible those matters which are outside the scope of Quality Circles. Circles
are, after all, chartered to work on work-related problems. They are not given
free reign to wander around stirring up hornets' nests. The activities of Quality
Circles encompass a different kind of work than most Circle members are

accustomed to, but it is, nonetheless, work. While the most successful Circles are granted a large degree of autonomy in selecting the problems they work on, they are also restricted from probing into areas which legitimately are outside their purview. Examples of such matters are: wages and salaries, interpersonal conflicts, grievances, and in general, anything which directly concerns a labor contract or which is in violation of laws or statutes.

Below is a sample statement of policies and procedures to provide general guidance in the operation of a Quality Circle program. It is included here not as an all encompassing model to be followed blindly, but rather as an example to be studied and modified as best suits your particular situation.

Procedure: Quality Circles Program

1.0 **Purpose**

    1.1 This procedure will define the policy and structure of Quality Circles within the organization.

2.0 **Policy**

    2.1 All employees are free to . . .

        2.1.1 Join or not join, drop out of or under some conditions return to a Circle in their work area.

        2.1.2 Suggest problems to Circles as potential topics for investigation and resolution.

    2.2 Management will . . .

        2.2.1 Be supportive of Circles by:

            Allowing time weekly for Circles to meet.

            Encouraging Circle members to attend scheduled Circle functions.

            Providing adequate meeting areas and materials for Circles to conduct effective meetings.

        2.2.2 Be participative in Circle actions by:

            Replying rapidly to Circle requests and, when necessary, giving detailed explanations to denied requests.

            Implementing approved Circle solutions expeditiously.

            Respecting the autonomy of Circles; e.g. not independently resolving a problem that a Circle is solving.

        2.2.3 Have the right to suggest problems to Circles and/or departments where new Circles may be formed.

2.3 Circles will . . .

    2.3.1 Be totally voluntary.

    2.3.2 Assure that each member has one vote.

    2.3.3 Follow techniques as described in Participant's Manual.

    2.3.4 Set up schedules for meeting and presentations within the framework of known company workloads.

    2.3.5 Collaborate on any work related problem pertaining to Quality of product/service and/or working conditions in the Circle area.

    2.3.6 Not address the following subjects:

Benefits and salaries

Matters requiring access to confidential information

Personnel-related decisions (e.g., who is hired, fired, promoted, etc.)

Designing new products

Personalities

    2.3.7 Have the right to accept/refuse problems submitted from any source.

    2.3.8 Identify, analyze and implement solutions to problems.

If implementation requires management approval, the Circle will present the problems and its requested solution to management for acceptance.

    2.3.9 Present periodic reviews to management on the progress of the Circle.

    2.3.10 Attempt to improve communications between all employees.

3.0 **Organization**

3.1 Quality Circles . . .

Are small groups of people usually 3 to 12 in size, who do similar work, and who voluntarily meet regularly to identify and analyze causes of problems in their work area, recommend their solutions to management and where possible, implement the solutions themselves.

3.2 Quality Circle Leader . . .

Is the immediate supervisor of the Circle members. He/She is responsible for the operation of the Circle and teaches Circle members in Quality Circle techniques. He/She works closely with the Facilitator. In decision-making, he/she votes only to break ties.

3.3 Quality Circle Facilitator . . .

Is responsible for the overall Quality Circle program. The Facilitator:

Trains Leaders and members

Maintains records

Coordinates Circle operations

Interfaces between Circles and company organizations and departments

Works closely with the Steering Committee

Is appointed by the Steering Committee

3.4 Steering Committee...

Is analogous to a Board of Directors.

Representatives are chosen from volunteers by management, from the major functions of the organization.

The Committee is responsible for establishing program policies, procedures, objectives and resources. They provide guidance and direction to the Quality Circle program within and outside of the organization. They incorporate Quality Circles throughout the organization. They also show their visibility by meeting regularly with the Facilitators and by attending management presentations.

Planning

Planning the implementation of Quality Circles is, without a doubt, the single most important facet of its application. Because Quality Circles have unequalled potential for effecting fundamental change in the management style of any organization, a myriad of questions must be answered to ensure their success. Every application will have some variations which no single plan can possibly encompass. A few of the most common questions will be presented here, and then we will offer an effective technique for drawing out the many specific details which should be addressed by any organization.

The first, and most basic, question for any management to answer is one of objectives. What do you want to achieve with Quality Circles? At first blush it might appear that this is a frivolous conjecture, but it is one of the most overlooked questions, and, at the same time, one of the first to be asked by potential members. The answer to the question of management's goals and objectives in starting Quality Circles will form the base of your introduction of Quality Circles to your people. In most organizations there seems to be little agreement on the answer to this question. Some managers are content to generalize their answers into a few very nebulous categories such as: "To improve communications," or "To create a quality awareness," or "To increase productivity," for example. These are all nice sounding objectives which do not say very much, but we get into trouble when someone asks

"What does that mean?" We may have heard and used these generalizations so frequently that we have begun to believe that they mean the same thing to everybody. They do not, of course, and we then fumble around trying to explain just what we mean. The more specific we try to be in our definitions, then the easier will be the task of convincing potential Circle members of our intentions. An additional benefit of such a statement is that it helps provide a measure of continuity in the face of management mobility.

Many other questions must be answered concerning the implementation of Quality Circles. These pertain to the structure, schedule, training, operation, funding and so forth. A practical approach to the identification of most of these questions has been utilized by a number of organizations. We will introduce that technique now, in the hope that it will help you to avoid needless pitfalls, mistakes and false starts.

The technique which many have found to be of great help in planning the implementation of Quality Circles is an iterative process, much like what Quality Circles use in their deliberations. In fact, it utilizes the five W's and an H which Circles are taught to use throughout their identification and analysis of problems (who, what, where, when, why and how).

At the top of a sheet of paper write the word "*Who.*" At the top of another sheet write the word "*What,*" and so on until you have all six words heading six sheets of paper. Then start writing down all the questions you have about Quality Circles in your organization on the page with the appropriate word at the top. Do not try to organize your questions any more than that at this time. What you are looking for is a multitude of ideas. Do not worry about duplications; there are bound to be some, and those may be the true keys to potential problems which you want to identify and resolve.

If this is going to be done before you have established any Quality Circle organization, ask anyone else who is interested to create his or her own list. If you have already established a Steering Committee, this is an ideal method of initiating everyone's participation in the planning stage. Typically, the more participation you can get at this early stage, the more participation you will enjoy in the weeks and months ahead.

The next iteration of this questioning process should take place before you attempt to answer the questions you just asked yourself. Pick any one of the six sheets and select any one of the questions you have written down. For instance, on the "*Who*" sheet you may have something like this:

Who

are circle members
leads the circle
is the Facilitator

monitors the circle's progress
keeps minutes of the meetings
trains the members
provides funding for circle meeting time
needs Quality Circles

Suppose you select the question "Who are circle members?" Write the word *Members* at the top of another sheet of paper and repeat the process for just the subject of Members. The difference is that now you ask yourself all the questions you can about Circle members, using the 5 W's and an H.

Members

who are they
why are they volunteers
what training will they get
where will they meet
when will they solve problems
how are they selected

When you feel you have exhausted all your questions, start to group the questions you have written on the various sheets. You can color code them so they are easier to identify, or use symbols. This procedure is not designed to be done in a quick, offhand manner. It takes some time and considerable effort to do it well. Many of your questions can be answered by doing some research among organizations which now have Quality Circles. This book, a consultant, and other information sources also may be helpful. In any case, this planning effort will be well worth the expenditure of time and energy as you go forward with your implementation of Quality Circles. One of the most important lessons to be learned from what is popularly known as the "Japanese Management Style" is the value of consensus in the planning stages of any effort. Do not be fearful of controversy in this process, as it is through the open exchange of ideas that you will arrive at the best method of implementing Circles in your organization.

Monitoring Circle Progress

When the circles are in place and operating, there will be a need to determine the extent to which those circles are successful. The key to a successful Quality Circle effort, after all, is that problems are being resolved and change is occurring. Without change, the process is simply an exercise that, in time, will disappear. Thus, it is vital that you monitor change or the lack thereof and provide this information to the Steering Committee and to management in general. To track this change, there are three things that must be done.

1. Develop measurable objectives

Throughout the past couple of chapters, we have touched repeatedly upon the importance of developing Quality Circle objectives. At this point, however, we will consider them again, this time from the perspective of using them as a guide to measuring circle success.

Some common objectives toward which Quality Circles work include:

- Reducing work-related costs
- Reducing the scrap and re-work rates
- Reducing absenteeism among employees
- Reducing turnover among employees
- Improving employee morale
- Improving house-wide communications
- Improving the quality of service or products
- Improving employee recruitment efforts
- Improving public/community relations
- Improving productivity

Each of these objectives is achievable through Quality Circles, and each of them is measurable. Thus, as a part of the objective-setting process, the Steering Committee needs to determine both the objectives desired and the measures to be used.

2. Take base-line measures

Obviously, if we are to assess future improvements, we first must measure the current situation. Typically, much of this information already is available: materials costs, wage and salary costs, scrap and re-work rates, absenteeism rates, turnover rates, reject rates (due to poor product quality), complaint rates (due to poor service), recruitment costs and time needed to fill open positions, and so on. However, special measures may be needed to assess some of the "softer" objectives. For example, employee morale, house-wide communications, and community relations may be measured by the number of employee grievances filed or the types of things said about the organization through the media, but it may also be useful to construct an opinion survey questionnaire which measures specific aspects of employee morale, perceptions of communication and cooperation, and public attitudes toward the organization. These measures, again, should be constructed and administered prior to initiation of the Quality Circles process.

3. Document on-going changes

The data provided by this information system will be used in four ways. The Steering Committee uses this information to monitor the overall effectiveness of the circle effort. The Facilitator and circle leader also use the data to manage the circle activities and operations. Third, this documentation can be used within the circle as a vehicle for recognition or a stimulus for involvement/ enthusiasm by reviewing progress and setting goals. Last, this empirical description of the circle and its activity is the most persuasive way to discuss the effort with critics and interested parties.

Tracking projects is the single most important measure because it is the problem resolution and change that drive this effort. The barometers used in tracking the projects are:

- Numbers of projects started.
- Numbers of projects completed.
- The average number of circle man-hours needed to complete a project.
- The average number of working days between the completion date and the implementation date.
- The average estimated value of the change per project.
- Verification of improvement made by the change.

Circle Effectiveness. Again, the effectiveness of each circle is best measured by tracking the projects and change. However, we have found it most helpful to follow the use of the problem solving process as an indicator. Not following the process is the first sign of a floundering circle. And, spending a great deal of time on any one step is another indication of trouble.

Leader Effectiveness. The leader is a key to the success of a Quality Circle. We have found that observations by the Facilitator and Steering Committee members is the best monitoring device. Facilitators attend many circle meetings. They meet with the leader prior to most meetings to insure planning for meetings, and a post circle meeting feedback process is established where a copy of a feedback sheet is presented to the leader while a second copy is kept on file by the Facilitator. A sample form is presented in Figure 1.

The feedback sheet serves as a behavior change tool and documentation of a leader's skills. The amount of feedback a leader can absorb is relatively small, so feedback is restricted to three positive comments and one comment on what action was counterproductive. The space for "additional comments" is used to suggest one area to work on, thereby improving at the next session.

Figure 1

Quality Circle Leader's Feedback

Feedback for: _____   _____

                                                     (Facilitator)

Session conducted on:_____

                   (Date)

Topic: _____

Positive Comments:	**Counter Productive Actions:**

Additional Comments:

As a rule, there is more of an effort on the leaders' part to modify their behavior to enhance the Quality Circle effectiveness when feedback and suggestions are given to them in writing rather than when the same feedback is given verbally.

Note that the leader effectiveness encompasses both process orientation and leadership style. Additionally, the facilitator talks with the participants to get another perspective of the leader's impact, or may ask them to complete a "leader rating scale" (Figure 2) to gain their perceptions.

Figure 2
Leader Rating Scale

Date _____   Leader _____

Time _____   Observer _____

Instructions: Rate the leader on all items which are applicable; draw a line through all items which do not apply. Use the following scale to indicate how well you evaluate his or her performance:

5 — superior
4 — above average
3 — average
2 — below average
1 — poor

Leadership Style and Personal Characteristics

To what degree did the leader:

_____ Show poise and confidence in speaking?
_____ Show enthusiasm and interest in the problem?
_____ Listen well to other participants?
_____ Manifest personal warmth and a sense of humor?
_____ Behave with objectivity, an open mind to all ideas?
_____ Create a supportive, cooperative atmosphere?
_____ Share functional leadership with other members?
_____ Behave democratically?

(over)

Preparation

To what degree:

_____ Were all physical arrangements cared for?
_____ Was the leader's preparation and grasp of the problem thorough?
_____ Were questions prepared to guide the discussion?
_____ Were members notifed and given adequate guidance for preparing?

Procedural and Interpersonal Leadership Techniques

To what degree did the leader:

_____ Put members at ease with each other?
_____ Introduce the problem so it was clear to all members?
_____ Guide the group to a thorough analysis of the problem before talking about solutions?
_____ Suggest an outline or pattern for group problem solving?
_____ Encourage members to modify the outline or agenda?
_____ State questions so they were clear to all members?
_____ Rebound questions to the group, especially if asking for an opinion?
_____ Facilitate mutual understanding?
_____ Keep the discussion on one point at a time?
_____ Provide the summaries needed to clarify, remind, and move forward?
_____ Encourage the group to evaluate all ideas and proposals?
_____ Equalize opportunity to participate?
_____ Stimulate imaginative and creative thinking?
_____ Control aggressive or dominant members with tact?
_____ Attempt to resolve misunderstandings and conflicts quickly but effectively?
_____ Test for consensus before moving to a new phase of problem solving?
_____ Keep complete and accurate records?
_____ See that plans were made to implement and follow-up on decisions?

Member Participation. Member participation and involvement is another dimension of an effective circle. Observation of the participants by the Facilitator is one measure of their involvement. We have also found that tracking attrition, attendance and tardiness has been helpful in predicting circle problems. There will always be a certain attrition rate, but we are interested in knowing whether we are losing a contributing member or someone who is not sincerely interested. When a member drops out of a circle (other than promotion, shift change, job change) the leader and facilitator rate the member as either a positive contributor or negative contributor. They then look at what the individual's commitment has been for attendance. Generally, a pattern shows early as to what is happening within an individual. Those members who are positive contributors stay with the program longer than the negative contributors. In fact, the negative members tend to drop out in the first few months. The chart in Figure 3 can be useful in tracking member attendance. Finally, the circle leader should use the "Participant Rating Scale" regularly to chart each member's performance in circle meetings (Figure 4).

Organization Support. Organization support is a general area that ranges from visits to circles by upper management to assistance in data gathering by support departments. To illustrate empirically the level of organization support, you might use the implementation data from tracking the projects and the following two indices.

1. Positive responses from people outside the circle divided by number of requests for assistance made by the circle.

$$\frac{+ \text{ Responses}}{\# \text{ Requests}}$$

2. The number of positive responses by others less the negative responses by others divided by the number of circles.

$$\frac{+ \text{ Responses less } - \text{ Responses}}{\# \text{ of Circles}}$$

Figure 3

_____ Quality Circle																	
Members	(month)						(month)						(month)				

Comments:

P — Present
A — Absent
T — Tardy
V — Vacation

Figure 4

Participant Rating Scale

Participant Rated: _____ Date: _____

1. Contribution to *content of the discussion* (well prepared, supplied important information, helped group reasoning, etc.):

    ____ Outstanding   Comments: _____
    ____ Excellent   _____
    ____ Average
    ____ Needs Improvement   _____
    ____ Needs Much Improvement   _____

2. Contribution to *efficient group procedure* (kept comments relevant, kept group on track, helped move things along, etc.):

    ____ Outstanding   Comments: _____
    ____ Excellent   _____
    ____ Average
    ____ Needs Improvement   _____
    ____ Needs Much Improvement   _____

3. Contribution to *social climate* of group (listened well, cooperative, group-oriented, open-minded, etc.):

    ____ Outstanding   Comments: _____
    ____ Excellent   _____
    ____ Average
    ____ Needs Improvement   _____
    ____ Needs Much Improvement   _____

(over)

4. Communication skills (speaks clearly, speaks concisely, addresses one point at a time, understands other members, etc.):

___ Outstanding   Comments: _____

___ Excellent   _____

___ Average

___ Needs Improvement   _____

___ Needs Much Improvement   _____

5. Value to the group in general:

___ Extremely Valuable   Comments: _____

___ Generally Valuable   _____

___ Average

___ Needs Improvement   _____

___ Needs Much Improvement   _____

How could this participant improve?

Each week the Facilitator may write a brief summary of a circle's meeting, and organizational support happenings are noted in left column for each reference (see Figure #5).

Figure 5

_____   _____

Quality Circle Leader   ⁄ Date

_____

Project

Organizational Support	Comments:
	_____
	Facilitator

(over)

Quality Circle Leader   Date

Project

Organizational Support	Comments:
	Facilitator

Generally, organizational support motivates a circle. It has frequently been noted that when a manager visits a group, the motivation of the group goes up. Also, the credibility of the program and the concept improves.

Another measure of organizational support is the amount of time it takes to implement changes recommended by the circles. This information is available on the Project Summary Sheet (Figure #6). Implementation time is also a key factor in the motivation of circle members. It is important that the people begin to *see* change as a result of their efforts.

Figure 6
Project Summary
_____ 19 _____
(Qtr)

Project: _____ Code Number:_____

Start Date: _____ Completed Date:_____

Implementation Date:_____Anticipated Implementation Date: _____

Cost: _____ Estimated Value: _____ Savings: _____

Project: _____ Code Number:_____

Start Date: _____ Completed Date:_____

Implementation Date:_____Anticipated Implementation Date: _____

Cost: _____ Estimated Value: _____ Savings: _____

(over)

Figure 6, Continued

Project:_____Code Number: _____

Start Date: _____ Completed Date:_____

Implementation Date:_____Anticipated Implementation Date: _____

Cost: _____ Estimated Value: _____ Savings: _____

Project:_____Code Number: _____

Start Date: _____ Completed Date:_____

Implementation Date:_____Anticipated Implementation Date: _____

Cost: _____ Estimated Value: _____ Savings: _____

Project:_____Code Number: _____

Start Date: _____ Completed Date:_____

Implementation Date:_____Anticipated Implementation Date: _____

Cost: _____ Estimated Value: _____ Savings: _____

Project:_____Code Number: _____

Start Date: _____ Completed Date:_____

Implementation Date:_____Anticipated Implementation Date: _____

Cost: _____ Estimated Value: _____ Savings: _____

Return on Investment. "What kind of a return are we getting on this effort?" is a valid question that is asked frequently for different reasons.

The best available facts and judgments should be used to answer this question. In considering this issue, however, it must also be kept in mind that there is a cost associated with the generation of accurate cost data and that not all issues can be reduced to cost and return figures.

To deal with this situation, the cost and return data generation can be turned over to an objective third party, the Controller. This may be done via two forms (Figure 7 and Figure 8). The forms serve the following functions:

1. provide project identification for cost analysis,
2. provide list of personnel to contact for cost analysis,
3. provide number of man-hours spent by Quality Circle members,
4. provide man-hours utilized outside the circle,
5. provide name of support activities and personnel required in the project,
6. provide a list of benefits of the project to measure for cost savings,
7. provide feedback to Facilitator on how Financial personnel are calculating cost savings of Quality Circle program,
8. provide cost analysis for Steering Committee.

Figure 7

Date: _____

To: _____Accounting_____ cc: _____

From: _____ _____

Subject: _Quality Circle Project_____ _____

Project:_____

_____

Project Code: _____ Start Date: _____ Completed Date: _____

Solutions/Conclusions: _____

_____

(over)

Implementation Steps:

Implementation Responsibility: _____
                                    Name   Telephone Number

Anticipated Implementation Date: _____ Implementation Date: _____

People to Contact for Cost Analysis Assistance:

1. _____   _____
            Name   Telephone Number

2. _____   _____
            Name   Telephone Number

3. _____   _____
            Name   Telephone Number

Areas of Anticipated Value

Costs – Circle Activity & Support Activity

Circle Costs: Support Activity to Contact: Manhours   Cost

_____   _____   _____   _____
    Manhours
_____   _____   _____   _____
    Manhours
_____

To: _____Facilitator_____ Date:_____

From: ___Accounting_____

Subject: ___Quality Circle Project_____

Total Estimated Value: _____

Total Costs: _____

Savings: _____

46

Figure 8

Project Code:_____ Sheet No. 2

Areas of Estimated Value:	Estimated Value:
1.	
2.	
3.	
4.	
5.	
6.	
7.	
8.	
9.	
10.	
Comments:	Total Estimated Value:

The form is completed by the Facilitator and submitted to Accounting upon implementation of changes recommended by a Quality Circle. Many of the benefits of Quality Circle projects are not easily measured with dollars, although they are definitely of value to the organization. The benefits are measured and recorded by the Accounting department and returned to the Facilitator.

Quality Circles should build an atmosphere in which a problem is viewed as a challenge to be dealt with positively and creatively. To do that, it is imperative that we deal from facts and data, not opinion. Therefore, documentation is key to the effectiveness of a Quality Circle concept. Additionally, to manage and monitor the effectiveness of a Quality Circle effort requires the same discipline. Although not all absolutes, empirical measures are effective monitoring points that let you know whether the process is meeting its stated objectives.

Summary

The success of Quality Circles depends heavily upon the three things discussed in this chapter. First, the Steering Committee must be comprised of the appropriate people, must think through carefully the charter of the Quality Circles, and must lay out a policy which specifies each element of the program. Second, careful planning must be used to ensure that each activity and element of the process is taken into account, and to put these things into an appropriate sequence. Finally, measureable objectives must be set, baseline measures taken, and then on-going records kept to monitor each circle's progress and to assess the effectiveness of the program. These three things obviously involve some time and paperwork, but the investment made in these things will be far surpassed by the returns gained through an effective Quality Circles program.

4

Skill Building

The Quality Circles Facilitator has two basic functions: structuring the program, and training the leaders and participants. Both functions are equally important. If the program is poorly structured and planned, it probably will be unsuccessful. Similarly, if the leaders and/or participants lack needed skills, then even the best structure and planning will be ineffective. Both elements — systems and skills — must exist if the Quality Circles program is to benefit the organization.

Accompanying this manual are two others: the Leader's Manual, and the Participant's Manual. The Participant's Manual presents information which circle participants need in order to understand what Quality Circles is all about, to be able to communicate effectively and work together well, to be able to analyze and solve problems efficiently, and to be able to present their action plans effectively to management. The Leader's Manual contains all of these things, plus instruction on styles of management, how to implement participative decision-making, and how to conduct an effective meeting.

It would be convenient and simple if we had only to give these manuals to the leaders and participants, ask them to read the material, and then set them to work in their Quality Circles. Unfortunately, things do not work that simply. There is a need for some formal classroom instruction to supplement these written materials, making sure that everyone understands the concepts discussed in the manuals and giving them a chance to practice a few of the skills taught there. Thus, as Facilitator, you must provide them with these instructional opportunities.

In this chapter, we will do three things. First, we will discuss some basic principles of adult learning — things you must understand if you are to teach circle leaders and participants effectively. Second, we will examine the circle leader seminar, mapping out the seminar procedures to enable you to more easily implement the course. Finally, we will study the circle participant seminar, again discussing ways in which it should be taught. All of this should make it simpler for you to help circle leaders and participants to develop the skills they need for effective participation.

Principles of Learning

Learning is a relatively complex process, consisting of a number of specific elements. These include:

- Acquiring new knowledges, attitudes, and skills.
- Retaining these new things over time.
- Putting these new things into action via changes in behavior.
- Effort to bring these elements about (that is, working to learn rather than sitting back passively waiting for it to happen).

In short, learning is an active process whereby we obtain new ideas and attitudes and develop new skills which improve our behaviors. We achieve such learning through our sensory experiences: by seeing things, hearing things, touching things, smelling things, and tasting things. Of these senses, the first two — seeing and hearing — are far and away the most important. However, learning is more long-lasting when all of the senses are involved, and when the learning experience is repeated.

The object of Quality Circles training, of course, is to cause new leaders and participants to acquire new knowledge, new attitudes, and new skills. To accomplish this, we need to communicate with them through their senses and to involve them actively in the process. However, there are some other principles of learning which are important, and these are presented below.

a. Adults must want to learn. Children will learn something because someone — a teacher, a parent — tells them to. Or, they will learn something to avoid getting a failing grade, even though the subject holds little interest for them. Adults however, will not learn something just because someone says they should; they must have a desire to learn a new skill or to acquire knowledge. In effect, adults are practical in their approach to learning: they want to know how the training is going to help them, now. They are probably not interested in something that may be of value years from now.

These principles illustrate how important it is that leaders and participants leave each learning situation with the feeling that they have gained something useful from it. In addition, they show why people quickly become impatient with too much theory or background:

they respond best if taught simply and directly the things they want to learn.

b. Adults learn by doing. Research has shown that if adults immediately practice what they have learned and continue to use it, long-term retention is much higher. If adults do not have opportunities to be involved actively in learning, within a year they will forget 50% of what they learned in a passive way — i.e., by reading or listening. In two years, they will have forgotten 80%. In fact, some studies indicate that within 24 hours they will have forgotten 50% of what they heard the previous day, and, within two weeks, an additional 25%. Adults can learn by listening and watching, but they learn more rapidly and with a higher level of retention if they are actively involved in the learning process. This explains why adults should be encouraged to discuss a problem, think out a solution, and practice a skill. Adults must have the opportunity to use what they learn before they forget it or dismiss it from their memory.

c. Adults learn by solving realistic problems. If the problems are not realistic or applicable to real life, adults will not learn from them. Practical, realistic problems should be presented.

d. People learn by making corrections. Adults relate their learning to what they already know. If the new knowledge does not fit in with previous knowledge they will probably reject or dismiss it. On the other hand, if the new information can be related to things they already know, they are more likely to understand and remember it. Thus, any new information or skills must be related to what the individuals already know.

e. Adults learn best in an informal environment. If the environment is too much like a classroom, adults will not learn as well. Many adults have unpleasant memories of their school days; others feel they have finished school, and they do not care to be reminded of it. Also, if the environment is too "school-like," adults are likely to think the whole situation is childish. Consequently, the meeting place should be set up as informally as possible. Arranging the chairs in a V or U and permitting smoking (if there are no regulations against it) helps remove the inhibiting classroom atmosphere.

f. People respond to a variety of teaching methods. They learn better if an idea is presented in many ways, or when the information reaches them through more than one sensory channel. Of course, the method used will depend on what is being taught and on the desired objectives.

g. Adults want guidance, not grades. True, adults want to know how they are doing, or what progress they are making. This is important to them, but grades or tests may be frightening. Adults tend to shy away from tests because of the fear of being humiliated or of not doing well. They may believe that they will not do well because they have been out of school too long, or that they are "too old to learn." Still, they want reassurance that they are making satisfactory progress. Adults can and will measure their own progress. However, many times the standards they set for themselves are too high, and they become discouraged. Sincere praise and guidance from the instructor will help prevent this.

h. People understand and retain information best when that information is organized. As we have seen, people look for relationships and then use those relationships to interpret and remember new things. Organized information, by definition, specifies relationships within the new facts so that the learners do not have to hunt for connections, and it facilitates memory by providing all of the connection keys they need. Disorganized information, by forcing them to hunt for relationships, increases the likelihood that the learners will either become confused or that they will be unable to find any relationships and, out of frustration, simply stop listening.

i. People understand and retain information best when that information is repeated. The more frequently we encounter cause-effect, similarity, proximity, or known-unknown relationships, the more imprinted upon our minds those relationships become. Thus, novice actors forget their lines, rookie quarterbacks forget their plays, and you get lost on your way home to your new house, all because they and you have not repeated the associations between information often enough. To promote understanding and memory of particularly important points, then, we must take care to repeat those points fairly often (just as television commercials repeat their points frequently) so that the learners remember them.

j. People understand and retain information best when that information has some emotional impact. As you think back over your life, what events do you remember best? The day you left home for the first time? The day someone close to you died? Probably you recall most vividly events that had a powerful emotional impact upon you — things that made you extremely happy, sad, frightened, and so on. Although it is unlikely that we can produce the same degree of emotional impact upon circle leader's and participants' emotions, we still can apply this principle when teaching. Through the use of vivid descriptions, emotional comparisons, dramatic stories, and other devices, we can involve their emotions and use that emotionalism to get them to remember the information we provide.

From this rather long list of principles come some objectives which we should keep in mind while training Quality Circle leaders and participants. Specifically, we want to:

- Motivate the leaders and participants to learn (probably not a major problem, since they volunteered to participate).
- Actively involve them in the learning process.
- Provide them with realistic problems.
- Help them to see relationships and draw connections.
- Create an informal environment.
- Use varied teaching and presentational methods which involve as many senses as possible.
- Present well-organized, personally meaningful information.
- Provide feedback on achieved learning.

It is toward these objectives that we will work as we implement the training seminars outlined below.

Leader Training

The leader training seminars, as we have seen, are provided for those supervisors and managers who are to lead Quality Circle groups. It may also be appropriate to invite non-leaders to attend these seminars; for example, supervisors who may become leaders when the process expands, members of the Steering Committee, interested members of top management, or the immediate superiors of the supervisors being trained.

The leader seminar is most effective with groups of 20 or fewer. If more than 20 leaders are to be trained, the total group should be split into two (or three, or four, etc.) groups, and two or more seminar sessions. Those split groups should be as heterogeneous as possible, and not consist of supervisors who see one another every day. The seminar activities are designed to promote communication among the attendees, and there is an advantage over time to having supervisors who rarely or never see one another learn about each other during these sessions.

Equipment needed for the seminars includes:

- Pads for taking notes
- Pens or pencils (for those who forget them)
- One copy of the *Quality Circle Leader's Manual* for each attendee
- Copies of handouts for each attendee
- Copies of the overhead transparencies
- An overhead transparency projector and screen
- An easel sheet/flip pad and/or a chalkboard
- Marking pens or chalk
- Extension cords (if needed)
- A spare projector bulb (just in case)

Accomodations for the seminar should consist of moveable chairs, either arranged around tables "classroom" style or "conference" style, or with attached desk arms. Attendees obviously will need something to write on during the seminar, but at the same time they will need to be able to rearrange themselves to participate in some of the activities.

There are four basic sections which can be incorporated into the leader training seminar. These include:

1. Participative leadership and conducting meetings
2. Effective communication skills
3. Effective problem-solving techniques
4. Procedural aspects of Quality Circles

Each of these sections requires approximately 4 hours of classroom instruction. However, well-trained supervisors may not need all four of these sections. Sections 1 and 2 often are presented as a part of supervisory effectiveness programs, so that only sections 3 and 4 may be necessary. Thus, the amount of training given circle leaders will be at least 4 (and probably 8) hours, and at most 16. These sessions may be offered in any number of ways: over a two-day period in which all four are covered consecutively; over a four-day period in which half-day sessions are offered each day; over a two-week period in which one day of instruction is given the first week, followed by a day of instruction the second week; or over a four-week period in which a half day of instruction is given each week. None of these is significantly better than the others, although leaders may become impatient during the four-week span. The key, however, is ease of scheduling for the organization. In short, set up a schedule that poses the least inconvenience for the organization.

Ultimately, you may wish to develop your own course content, adapted specifically to your own organization. To help you initially, however, the course outlines below and corresponding activites are presented.

I. Participative Leadership and Conducting Meetings

I. Introduction
   A. Facilitator introduces self, asks each person in room to introduce and tell a little about himself/herself.
   B. Facilitator lists session objectives:
      1. To acquaint participants with Quality Circles
      2. To have participants understand how Quality Circles will be implemented in this organization
      3. To have participants examine their own style(s) of leadership
      4. To teach participants techniques for participative leadership
      5. To provide participants with basic skills in running meetings
   C. Facilitator presents session agenda
      1. Discussion of Quality Circles concept
      2. Distribution of Quality Circles documents
      3. Study of leadership styles and a self-test of own style
         — Break —
      4. Discussion of participative leadership
      5. Discussion and activity in how to conduct an effective meeting
         — End of session —

II. The Quality Circles Concept
   A. Definitions of Quality Circles: "Groups of people who meet to define, analyze, and solve work-related problems"
   B. Objectives of Quality Circles (see page 6 of Participant's Manual)
   C. Brief History of Quality Circles
   D. How the Program is Structured (use overhead transparency of chart on page 9 of Participant's Manual)
   E. How the Program is Implemented (see stages in Chapter I of this book)

III. Quality Circles in This Organization
   A. Who Plays each Circle Role (Steering Committee Members, Facilitator, etc.)
   B. Objectives Selected by Steering Committee
   C. Policy Concerning Quality Circles (hand out any policy written by Steering Committee)
   D. Time Table for Circle Events

IV. Styles of Leadership
   A. Three Components of Leadership Style: Assumptions, Power, and Communication
   B. Assumptions About People (have participants complete questionnaire on pp. 3-5 of Leader's Manual)
       1. Theory X leadership (scores mean: 0-5 is low; 6-10 is medium; over 10 is high)
       2. Theory Y leadership (0-5 low; 6-10 medium; over 10 high)
       3. Brief lecture on the Pygmalion Effect. Have participants discuss ways in which assumptions and expectations are communicated. Apply these principles to QC meetings.
   C. Use of Power (see pp. 10-14 in Leader's Manual)
       1. Democratic leadership
       2. Autocratic leadership
       3. Laissez-faire leadership
   D. Types of Communication
       1. Communication Styles (see pp. 14-17 in Leader's Manual)
       2. Communication Profiles (have participants complete questionnaire on p. 19, then compare answers with profile on p. 21. Discuss importance and methods of gaining employee input concerning communication preferences)
   E. Summary: Where Leadership Style Comes From (p. 22) (Have participants discuss which style seems most valued in this organization, and why they feel that way)

— Break —

V. Participative Leadership
   A. Definition
       1. Means shared responsibility for problems and solutions
       2. Does not mean "employees run the store," or organization becomes a democracy

B. Advantages of Participative Leadership (p. 25, Leader's Manual)

C. Cautions Concerning Participative Leadership (pp. 27-29)

D. Promoting Participation
   1. Non-directed questions
   2. Directed questions
   3. Re-directed questions

E. Problems of Participation
   1. Conflict (pp. 33-35)
   2. Criticism (pp. 35-36)
   3. Coalitions (pp. 36-37)
   4. Group think (p. 37)
   5. Hidden Agendas (p. 38)

VI. Conducting Meetings

A. Amount of Control Provided (pp. 42-43)

B. Preparing for Meetings

C. Conducting Meetings (use NASA problem on following page as simulation for participant activity)

D. Analyzing Meetings (hand out "Leader Rating Scale" and "Participant Rating Scale" and have them apply it to their own group session in solving NASA problem)

E. Processing Meetings (to illustrate how to process meetings, conduct discussion of this seminar session: what should they have done more of, less of? what did they like, not like? what helped them most, least? Then, how can this sort of discussion occur at the end of Quality Circle meetings?)

VII. Conclusion

A. Review of Things Covered in Seminar

B. Final Questions & Answers

C. Announcement of Next Event in QC Process

— End of Session —

The NASA Problem

Purpose

To illustrate the principles of setting criteria for solutions and ranking alternatives.

Procedures

1. Break participants into groups of 5-7 people
2. Select a leader in each group. However, do not describe what he/she is to do. Just appoint that person "leader."
3. Distribute a copy of the NASA Problem shown on the next page to every member of the group.
4. Allow time for everyone to read the problem, then begin discussion.
5. Allow discussion to continue until all groups have reached a decision, or until 20 minutes is up.

Principles Illustrated

After the exercise, a brief discussion may be used to point out the following:

1. The need for leadership to structure group proceedings
2. The need for setting criteria before attempting to make choices
3. The sharing of the leadership role
4. Visible styles of leadership (autocratic, democratic)
5. Ways of arriving at a decision (vote, discussion, etc.)

The NASA Problem

Imagine your group is a space crew originally scheduled to meet with a mother ship on the lighted surface of the moon. Due to mechanical difficulties, however, your ship was forced to land some 200 miles from the meeting point. During landing, much of the equipment aboard was damaged. Since survival depends on reaching the mother ship, the most critical items available must be chosen for the 200-mile trip. Below are listed the items left undamaged and intact after landing. Your task as a group is to rank order them in terms of their importance to your crew in allowing them to reach the rendezvous point. Place the number 1 by the most important item, the number 2 by the second most important, and so on, through number 15, the least important. Again, since the decisions you reach affect the lives of every group member, consensus must be reached; a unanimous decision must be made.

____ Box of matches   ____ Parachute silk

____ Food Concentrate   ____ Life raft

____ 50 feet of nylon rope   ____ Portable heating unit

____ Two .45 caliber pistols   ____ Magnetic compass

____ Signal flares   ____ One case dehydrated milk

____ 5 gallons of water   ____ Two 100 pound tanks of oxygen

____ Solar-powered FM receiver-   ____ First-aid kit with injection
transmitter   needles

____ Stellar map (of the moon's constellations)

Answers: NASA Problem

_15_ Box of matches

_4_ Food concentrate

_6_ 50 feet of nylon rope

_8_ Parachute silk

_13_ Portable heating unit

_11_ Two .45 caliber pistols

_12_ One case dyhydrated milk

_1_ Two 100 pound tanks of oxygen

_3_ Stellar map

_9_ Life raft

_14_ Magnetic Compass

_2_ 5 gallons of water

_10_ Signal flares

_7_ First-aid kit

_5_ Solar-powered FM receiver-transmitter

Leader Rating Scale

Instructions: Rate the group leader on each item that applies; simply mark an X for items that do **not** apply. Use the following scale to indicate how well the leader performed in each area.

5 = Outstanding 4 = Good 3 = Average 2 = Below Average 1 = Poor

1. **Leadership Style:** How effectively did the leader:

   ____ Show enthusiasm and interest in the project at hand?

   ____ Listen well to the group members?

   ____ Show personal concern for the group members?

   ____ Act objectively, with an open mind to all ideas?

   ____ Create a supportive, cooperative atmosphere?

   ____ Share functional leadership with other members?

   ____ Behave democratically?

II. **Leadership Preparation:** How effectively did the leader:

   ____ Care for the physical arrangements?

   ____ Prepare for and have a grasp of the problem at hand?

   ____ Have questions prepared to guide the discussion?

   ____ Notify members in advance and guide them in preparing?

III. **Leadership Techniques:** How effectively did the leader:

   ____ Put members at ease with each other?

   ____ Introduce the problem so it was clear to everyone?

   ____ Make sure the problem had been analyzed before solutions were discussed?

   ____ Make sure the group followed a logical pattern of problem-solving?

   ____ Facilitate mutual understanding?

_____ Encourage all group members to participate?

_____ Control over-talkative members with tact?

_____ Make sure everyone agreed before moving on to a new phase of problem-solving?

_____ Keep the discussion on track, and on one point at a time?

_____ Stimulate creativity and imaginative thinking?

_____ Encourage the group to evaluate thoroughly ideas and proposals?

_____ Make sure that complete and accurate records were kept?

_____ Make sure that everyone clearly understands their duties before the next meeting?

How could the leader improve?

Participant Rating Scale

Participant Rated: _____ Date: _____

1. Contribution to *content of the discussion* (well prepared, supplied important information, helped group reasoning, etc.):

   ____ Outstanding   Comments: _____
   ____ Excellent
   ____ Average   _____
   ____ Needs Improvement
   ____ Needs Much Improvement   _____

2. Contribution to *efficient group procedure* (kept comments relevant, kept group on track, helped move things along, etc.):

   ____ Outstanding   Comments: _____
   ____ Excellent
   ____ Average   _____
   ____ Needs Improvement
   ____ Needs Much Improvement   _____

3. Contribution to *social climate* of group (listened well, cooperative, group-oriented, open-minded, etc.):

   ____ Outstanding   Comments: _____
   ____ Excellent
   ____ Average   _____
   ____ Needs Improvement
   ____ Needs Much Improvement   _____

(over)

4. Communication skills (speaks clearly, speaks concisely, addresses one point at a time, understands other members, etc.):

_____ Outstanding   Comments: _____
_____ Excellent   _____
_____ Average   _____
_____ Needs Improvement   _____
_____ Needs Much Improvement _____

5. Value to the group in general:

_____ Extremely Valuable   Comments: _____
_____ Generally Valuable   _____
_____ Average   _____
_____ Needs Improvement   _____
_____ Needs Much Improvement _____

How could this participant improve?

II. Effective Communication

I. Introduction
  A. Welcome to participants; introduction of guests
  B. Presentation of session objectives
    1. To increase participants' understanding of the nature of communication
    2. To improve participants' perception and listening skills
    3. To improve participants' ability to recognize and deal with verbal communication problems
    4. To increase participants' understanding of group process
  C. Overview of session agenda
    1. Study the Nature of Communication
    2. Study Listening Problems and Skills
    — Break —
    3. Study Verbal Barriers and How to Deal with Them
    4. Study the Dynamics of Groups

II. The Nature of Communication (pp. 19-22 in Participant's Manual)
  A. Do "One-Way and Two-Way Communication" exercise on next page.
  B. Discuss what made descriptions of the figures helpful or not helpful (for example, beginning with an overview of what the figure is, moving methodically step-by-step, etc.)
  C. Discuss what listening techniques (if any) participants used as they tried to draw the figures.
  D. Present the nature of communication (use model on p. 21 as overhead transparency to illustrate process and parts).

III. Effective Listening
  A. Read "bus driver" story; ask for answers; discuss principle.
  B. Distribute copies of "The Story"; ask participants to read it and then answer each statement. When they are done, discuss the role of assumptions in communication.
  C. Have participants complete the listening quiz (pp. 23-25 in Participant's Manual).
  D. Present the poor listening habits (pp. 25-26).
  E. Have participants take part in the "Paraphrasing" exercise.
  F. Review good listening habits (p. 27).
— Break —

One-Way and Two-Way Communication

Purposes

1. To demonstrate the concept of feedback
2. To demonstrate the concept of process

Procedures

1. Ask for a volunteer from the group.
2. Have the volunteer come to the front of the group. Hand him Figure I and ask him to look at it for a minute.
3. Give the group the following instructions:

   "Take out a piece of paper. (Volunteer's name) will describe for you a geometric figure. Your task is to draw that figure from his/her description. Do not ask any questions or give any feedback (groaning, laughing, etc.) while he/she is talking."

4. Ask the volunteer to face the front wall of the room with his/her back to the group. Tell him/her to take as much time as he/she needs describing the figure. Tell him/her to begin.
5. While the volunteer is speaking, time the length of the description. When he/she has finished, record the following:

   A. Time needed to complete description

   B. Volunteer's estimate of the number of figures each group member, on the average, drew accurately.

   C. Group members' estimate, on the average, of how many of the five figures they drew correctly.

6. Ask for another volunteer and repeat the entire process, except this time have the volunteer face the group so that he or she can perceive their nonverbal responses. Again, note length of description of the Figure (Figure II in this instance), volunteer's estimate of group accuracy, and group estimate of their own accuracy.
7. Ask for yet another volunteer. Give him or her Figure III and ask him or her to describe it, but this time allow free communication. Group members may interrupt whenever they like, asking whatever questions occur to them. The only restriction is that, as in the previous conditions, the volunteer may not use his or her hands to "draw" the figures in the air. Again time the length of the descriptions and note the accuracy estimates of the volunteer and group.

8. Draw the three figures on the blackboard or show them on the overhead, and have the group determine how many figures they drew correctly. To be judged correct, each figure (box) must be both shaped and positioned correctly. Record accuracy counts (on the average) for each of the three figures.

Principles Illustrated

1. Feedback increases understanding (accuracy counts should increase across the three conditions).
2. Feedback slows communication (length of time should have increased in each situation).
3. Feedback increases listener confidence (group accuracy estimates should increase across the three conditions).
4. Feedback may increase speaker confidence if he perceives understanding on the part of his receivers, or it may decrease confidence if he perceives they are confused. Accuracy estimates will indicate which occurred here.

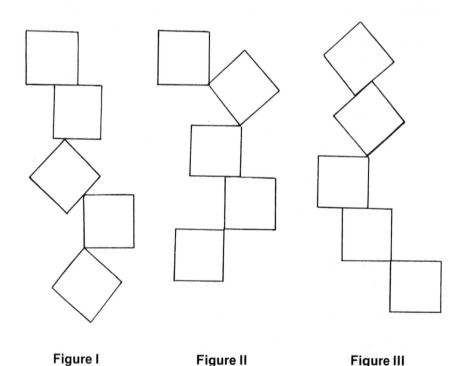

Figure I   **Figure II**   **Figure III**

Listening

Purpose
To identify weak points in individual's listening skills.

Procedure
1. Without warning begin a meeting by asking the group this question:

    "You are driving a bus down a country road. You come to a stop sign and turn left. Then go for two miles and at the fork in the road curve to the right. Travel down this road for eight miles and immediately after a bridge turn right again. Then, proceed for about six city blocks and make a left turn. Go until the road ends and turn right and in one mile make another right turn. How old is the bus driver?"

2. Wait for answers. Some may pick it up right away: however, often it takes people a few readings before they recognize the "You" in the question. The answer will, of course, be whatever age the listener is.

Principle Illustrated:
We often miss important and obvious detail because of poor listening habits.

The Story

Purpose
To illustrate how assumptions lead to potentially incorrect conclusions.

Procedures
1. Distribute a copy of "The Story" to everyone. Have them read it and answer the questions.
2. Ask them to report their answers to each question. The correct answers are:

    1.-? (Don't know if businessman was the owner)
    2.-? (Don't know if there was a robber; could have been the landlord demanding money for overdue rent)
    3.-F
    4.-? (Don't know if owner was a man)
    5.-? (Don't know who scooped up contents, or who ran away)
    6.-T
    7.-? (Don't know who scooped up contents or ran away)
    8.-? (Don't know if cash register contained money, although it is true story does not say how much)

9.-? (Don't know if there was a robber)

10.-? (Could be 4 or more)

11.-? (Don't know if man dashed out of store; story says a "man sped away"; could have been person driving getaway car for robber who was still in store)

Principles Illustrated

1. Our tendency to make assumptions based on incomplete information.
2. Our tendency to use labels which carry stereotypes ("man" is "owner").

The Story

A businessman had just turned off the lights in the store when a man appeared and demanded money. The owner opened a cash register. The contents of the cash register were scooped up and the man sped away. A member of the police force was notified promptly.

Statements About the Story

1. A man appeared after the owner had turned off his store lights. T F ?

2. The robber was a *man*. T F ?

3. The man did not demand money. T F ?

4. The man who opened the cash register was the owner. T F ?

5. The store owner scooped up the contents of the register and ran away. T F ?

6. Someone opened the cash register. T F ?

7. After the man who demanded the money scooped up the contents of the cash register, he ran away. T F ?

8. While the cash register contained money, the story did *not* state *how much*. T F ?

9. The robber demanded money of the owner. T F ?

10. The story concerns a series of events in which only three persons are referred to: The owner of the store, a man who demanded money, and a member of the police force. T F ?

11. The following events in the story are true: someone demanded money, a cash register was opened, its contents were scooped up, and a man dashed out of the store. T F ?

Paraphrasing

Purpose
1. To illustrate how commonly misunderstandings occur.
2. To make the group members more sensitive to other's statements.

Procedures
1. Divide the group in half to form two separate groups.
2. Give them the following instructions:

   "Your task as a group is to reach a decision on the question "What is the biggest problem this organization faces today?" The rules of this discussion are these. First, before you make a statement of your own, you must paraphrase the statement made just before yours. That is, you must tell what that statement meant to you before you go on to say what is on your mind. Second, your paraphrase must be approved by the preceding speaker. He must either agree that he meant what you said he meant, or he must clarify his meaning so that you can paraphrase it correctly before you proceed. So every statement must begin with a paraphrase of the preceding statement, and that paraphrase must be approved by the preceding speaker before you can proceed." After handling questions, start the discussions.
3. After about twenty minutes, stop the discussions and have the group members return to their places.

Principles Illustrated
Upon completion of the exercise, a brief discussion may be used to point out the following:
1. Frequency of misunderstanding: did paraphrases often have to be corrected?
2. Difficulty in listening: was it hard to focus on a statement and plan your own statement at the same time?
3. Surface meaning: were paraphrases given that sounded similar to the original statement, but which may have meant something different?

IV. Effective Sending
   A. Review the verbal sending problems (pp. 28-31 in Participant's Manual)
   B. Have the participants take part in the "Group Conformity" exercise (note: you will need to speak with the "deviant" during the break, explaining to him or her the role to be played).

C. At the end of the exercise, use the experience to talk about the following:
1. Nonverbal communication: did people treat the deviant differently than other members by looking more at him/her? Leaning toward or away from him/her? Making gestures? What did nonverbal communication reveal about members' feelings during the experience?
2. Norms and conformity: how did the group try to get the deviant "back in line?" (see pp. 46-47)
3. Group roles: did different members seem to take different roles during the discussion? (see pp. 49-51)
4. What motivational problems (hostility, defensiveness) occurred during the discussion? (see pp. 70-81)
5. How could a group leader have made this a more productive discussion?

V. Conclusion
A. Review everything covered in the session.
B. Answer any questions.
C. Announce future events.
— End of session —

Group Conformity

Purpose

To illustrate how majority members respond to group deviants.

Procedures

1. Prior to the meeting, meet with one group member. Instruct him or her that he or she is to be a group deviant, that the group will be given a "Who Should be Saved?" problem, and that his/her job is to keep the group from reaching consensus. Thus, when the group seems to be settling on one choice, the deviant should choose someone else and hold out at all costs. You may even discuss with him/her possible arguments to use in support of other alternatives.
2. When the meeting begins, give the group the story with the passenger list.

3. Tell the group their task is to choose an individual to be saved and they have only 20 minutes to make the decision. Note, however, that the choice must be unanimous; no voting is allowed. Begin the discussion.

"Several people are marooned on a small yacht in the South Pacific. The boat has just come through a violent storm, leaving it leaking and without radio communication. Unkown to the passengers, a nuclear test is scheduled in this area within the hour. A small seaplane has landed alongside and the pilot has advised them of the situation. There is no hope that a large-scale rescue will work. The pilot has no radio contact either, only he can fly the plane, and he can carry only one additional passenger. The yacht cannot be towed. The bombing is deadly and too far-reaching for anyone but those on the plane to escape.

Your job is to determine who will be saved. You must decide as a group which one of the following passengers should be allowed to go with the pilot."

1. The captain of the yacht.
2. A little boy.
3. A U.S. Senator.
4. A grandmother.
5. A university professor of agricultural science.
6. A brilliant artist.
7. A young doctor.
8. A prominent religious leader.
9. A leader of revolutionary forces in a small developing country.
10. A used car salesman.
11. A farmer.
12. A policeman.

III. Effective Problem Solving

I. Introduction
   A. Welcome participants; introduce guests
   B. State objectives of training session:
      1. To have participants understand the problem-solving process.
      2. To give participants basic skills for discovering and analyzing problems.
      3. To teach participants techniques for gathering and displaying information.

4. To teach participants techniques for identifying causes.
5. To show participants how to generate new ideas.
6. To determine criteria for judging possible solutions.
7. To teach participants how to structure action plans.

C. Outline the agenda for the session.
   1. An overview of problem-solving
   2. Identifying problems
   3. Gathering and displaying information
   — break —
   4. Identifying causes
   5. Suggesting solutions
   6. Evaluating solutions
   7. Developing action plans

II. Initiating Problem-Solving
   A. The problem-solving phases
   B. Identifying problems
      1. Listing problems (have participants suggest problems for QC group discussion by asking, "What problems does this organization have now?").
      2. Analyzing work (have participants complete "Flow Process Chart" exercise, either using "eating at McDonald's" as process for analysis, or suggesting one of your own).
      3. Gathering information (review techniques given on pp. 91-95 of Participant's Manual).
      4. Displaying information (using Flow Process Chart data from point 2 above, complete "Displaying Information" exercise).
      5. Selecting problems (present criteria, pp. 114-115; review areas excluded from QC consideration by Steering Committee).

— Break —

III. Seeking Causes
   A. Brainstorming (review rules, pp. 123-126).
   B. Fishbone diagramming (have participants complete "Fishbone Diagramming" exercise for problem selected from list produced by point II.B.1. above).
   C. Selecting causes (have group select one or more important causes of problem through discussion).

IV. Developing Actions
   A. Methods of generating ideas (review brainstorming, silent idea generation, survey sampling on pp. 123-129).
   B. Evaluating solutions (review criteria & decision balance sheet, pp. 138-140).
   C. Choosing a solution (review decision-making methods, pp. 140-146).
   D. Action planning (distribute Action Plan sheet; review).

V. Quality Circles Meetings: Schedule of Events
   A. Meeting 1: Identifying problems and brainstorming
   B. Meeting 2: Analyzing work; flow process charting
   C. Meeting 3: Gathering information; assign responsibilities
   D. Meeting 4: Displaying information
   E. Meeting 5: Selecting problem; fishbone diagramming causes
   F. Meeting 6: Selecting causes
   G. Meeting 7: Brainstorming solutions; selecting most practical
   H. Meeting 8 and continuing: Developing actions

VI. Conclusion
   A. Summary of things covered
   B. Question and answer
   C. Announcement of next event(s)

Flow Process Chart

Purpose

To familiarize group members with the use of Flow Process Charts.

Procedure

1. Hand out blank flow process charts to each member of the group.
2. Instruct them to chart the job of "Eating at McDonald's" starting from the parking to returning to the parking lot.
3. Allow them fifteen minutes, then ask them to stop.
4. Have everyone compare their charts, then compare those charts with the example we have charted on the following page.

Principles Illustrated

1. Effective use of Flow Process Charts
2. The several ways one simple process may be charted.

Current Process _____

Proposed Process _____

Flow Process Chart

Summary Chart

	Real	Ideal	Difference
O Operation			
T Transportation			
I Inspection			
D Delay			
S Storage			
Distance			
Time			

Job charted: _____

_____

Performed by: _____

Charted by:_____

Process begins _____

Process ends _____

Event	Type	Dist.	Time	Notes
1	O T I D S			
2	O T I D S			
3	O T I D S			
4	O T I D S			
5	O T I D S			
6	O T I D S			
7	O T I D S			
8	O T I D S			
9	O T I D S			
10	O T I D S			
11	O T I D S			
12	O T I D S			
13	O T I D S			
14	O T I D S			
15	O T I D S			
16	O T I D S			
17	O T I D S			

Example Flow Process Chart

Current Process _____

Page __1__ of __1__

Date___10/8/81___

Proposed Process _____

Flow Process Chart

Summary Chart

	Real	Ideal	Difference
O Operation	8		
T Transportation	4		
I Inspection	3		
D Delay	2		
S Storage	0		
Distance	228 ft	ft	ft
Time	23 min		

Job Charted: __Eating at McDonald's__

_____

Performed by: __Customer__

Charted by: __McDonald's Employee__

Process begins __In the parking lot__

Process ends__In the parking lot__

Event	Type	Dist.	Time	Notes
1 Get out of car	**O** T I D S		10 sec	
2 Walk into McDonald's	O **T** I D S	90 ft	90 sec	Distance varies depending on available parking
3 Read the menu	O T **I** D S		20 sec	
4 Stand in line	O T I **D** S		5 min	
5 Order food	**O** T I D S		35 sec	
6 Wait for food	O T I **D** S		2 min	
7 Receive food	O T **I** D S		2 sec	
8 Pay for food	**O** T I D S		30 sec	
9 Walk to seating area	O **T** I D S	30 ft	30 sec	
10 Choose table	O T **I** D S		10 sec	
11 Sit down	**O** T I D S		5 sec	
12 Eat food	**O** T I D S		10 min	
13 Get up	**O** T I D S		5 sec	
14 Walk to garbage can	O **T** I D S	18 ft	18 sec	
15 Deposit garbage	**O** T I D S		5 sec	
16 Walk out to car	O **T** I D S	90 ft	90 sec	
17 Get in car	**O** T I D S		10 sec	

Displaying Information

Purpose

To teach alternative ways of displaying gathered data.

Procedures

1. Divide total group into twos or threes.
2. Tell everyone to take out completed Flow Process Charts from earlier exercise.
3. Give each pair or trio a different task to perform, selecting from the list below:
   - Develop a check sheet indicating the number of times each type of event occurs, and then construct a Pareto chart showing the percentage of the total number of events each type of event comprises.
   - Develop a histogram showing the amount of time, in total, each type of event requires out of the total time taken by the charted process.
   - Develop a pie chart showing the percentage of time in the total process each type of event requires.
   - Develop a line graph which, across the bottom (the X axis), charts the first five events, the second five events, the third five events, and the fourth five events, and up the side (the Y axis) charts the number of seconds. Then draw lines indicating two things: the amount of time spent performing Operations during each five-event block, and the amount of time spent performing Delays during each five-event block.
4. Have each pair or group present their charts to the entire group, explaining what they did and what the chart means.

Principles Illustrated

1. Methods of displaying data
2. Usefulness of these methods in understanding and explaining information.

Fishbone Diagramming

Purpose

To teach the use of the fishbone diagram technique for identifying causes.

Procedures

1. Select a problem faced by the organization.
2. Write that problem at the "head" of the fishbone.

3. Review rules for brainstorming:
   a. Ideas are expressed freely, without taking turns or waiting for permission to speak.
   b. No criticism can be expressed (and no positive statements of evaluation, such as "that's a good idea," can be given).
   c. Wild ideas are encouraged.
   d. Hitching on to others' ideas is encouraged as a means of coming up with own ideas.
4. Appoint a recorder to write down ideas on the blackboard or easel sheet.

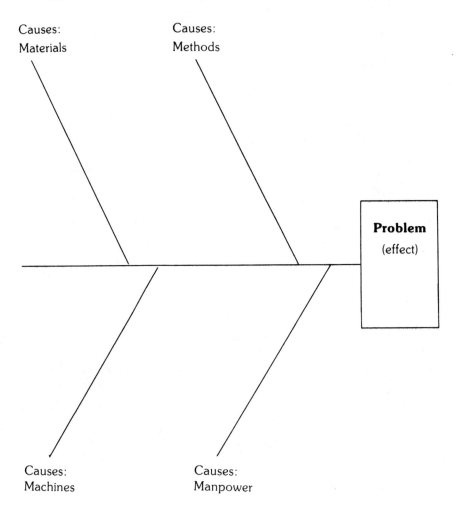

Causes:
Materials

Causes:
Methods

Problem
(effect)

Causes:
Machines

Causes:
Manpower

5. Allow 10 to 15 minutes for the group to brainstorm possible causes, taking one category of cause (Methods, Manpower, etc.) at a time.

Principles Illustrated
1. Improvements in efficiency brought about by fishbone diagram categories.
2. Techniques of brainstorming.
3. Need for decision-making to select most important causes once brainstorming is over.

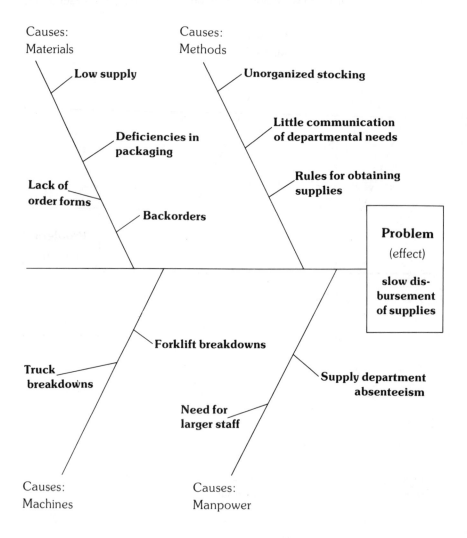

Causes: Materials

Causes: Methods

Low supply

Unorganized stocking

Deficiencies in packaging

Little communication of departmental needs

Lack of order forms

Rules for obtaining supplies

Backorders

Problem
(effect)

slow disbursement of supplies

Forklift breakdowns

Truck breakdowns

Supply department absenteeism

Need for larger staff

Causes: Machines

Causes: Manpower

IV. Quality Circle Procedures

I. Introduction
   A. Welcome participants; introduce guests
   B. State session objectives
       1. To clarify procedural elements of circles process
       2. To discuss potential problems or concerns
       3. To schedule future events
   C. Overview session agenda
       1. Lay out the sequence of events for the next several weeks
       2. Distribute and discuss various reporting and review forms
       3. Handle questions and answers

II. Sequence of Events
   (Here, present plan for implementation developed by Steering Committee, discuss it step by step, and lay out specific time tables as much as possible.)

III. Reporting Forms
   (Give each participant a copy of each form, and then take them one at a time and discuss how they are to be completed, how often they are to be done, and to whom they are to be sent.)

IV. Questions and Answers
   (Deal with matters arising. As much as possible, use Quality Circles techniques, such as brainstorming, action planning, and so on to arrive at answers or solutions to participant concerns.)

V. Conclusion
   A. Review all matters covered.
   B. Announce events scheduled next (usually the first Quality Circles leaders' meeting).

This session may require less than four hours; however, a half-day should be set aside for the session in case a great deal of discussion or concern occurs.

Participant Training

When leader training is completed, participant training occurs. This training involves two basic steps: classroom training for the participants, followed by training during the initial Quality Circle meetings. The classroom training should provide an introduction to the concept and process, and some basic skills in effective communications. The circle training then should teach problem-solving skills in conjunction with the work actually being done by the circle itself.

Participant training, like leader training, is most effective with groups of 25 or fewer (although it is possible to train larger groups if necessary). Thus, several training sessions may need to be given if large numbers of participants are being trained. To the greatest extent possible, members of QC groups should attend these sessions together. However, as with the leader training, circle groups from as wide a variety of departments as possible should attend. Again, the seminar activities are designed to promote communication and understanding among the attendees, and it ultimately is beneficial to bring together people who do not normally see or interact with one another. These training sessions may also be attended by the Steering Committee, interested members of management, and circle leaders (who should observe the session, but not participate actively).

The equipment and accommodations needed for the session are the same as in the leader training seminars. The total amount of classroom training required is 4 hours, which may be taught in a single half-day, or may be offered in two 2-hour sessions or four 1-hour sessions. Again, ease of scheduling is the most important consideration. The course outline below presents the content and activities involved in the participant training, and suggests breaking points at the end of each hour of instruction, thus making it easier for you to adapt to 4-hour, 2-hour, or 1-hour schedules. Ultimately, you may want to develop your own course outline and materials.

Participant Training Session(s)

I. Introduction
   A. Facilitator introduces self, asks each person in room to introduce self.
   B. Facilitator lists session objectives.
      1. To acquaint participants with Quality Circles.
      2. To have participants understand how circles will be implemented

in this organization.
3. To increase participants' understanding of the nature of communication.
4. To improve participants' perception and listening skills.
5. To acquaint participants with some of the difficulties involved in working in groups.

C. Facilitator previews session agenda
1. Discussion of Quality Circles concept
2. Explanation of Quality Circles process
3. Study of the nature of communication
4. Study of listening problems and skills
5. Study of group decision-making problems and skills

II. The Quality Circles Concept
A. Definition of Quality Circles: "Groups of people who meet to define, analyze, and solve work-related problems."
B. Objectives of Quality Circles (see p. 6, Participant's Manual).
C. Brief history of Quality Circles.
D. How the program is structured (same transparency as used in leader training).
E. How program is implemented.

III. Quality Circles in this Organization
A. Who plays each circle role
B. Objectives selected by Steering Committee
C. Policy concerning Quality Circles
D. Time table for circle events
— one hour —

IV. The Nature of Communication
A. Do "One-Way and Two-Way Communication" exercise.
B. Discuss what made descriptions of figures helpful or not helpful.
C. Discuss what listening techniques participants used.
D. Present nature of communication.
— one hour —

V. Effective Listening
   A. Read "bus driver" story; discuss.
   B. Distribute copies of "The Story"; have participants answer and discuss.
   C. Have participants complete listening quiz (pp. 23-25 in manual).
   D. Present the poor listening habits (pp. 25-26).
   E. Have participants take part in the "Paraphrasing" exercise.
   F. Review good listening habits (p. 27).
— one hour —

VI. Effective Sending
   A. Review the verbal sending problems (pp. 28-31 in Participant's Manual).
   B. Have participants take part in the "NASA" problem, working in their own QC groups. Appoint one of them to act as leader.
   C. When all groups have finished, distribute "Leader Rating Scale" and "Participant Rating Scale" and have them apply it to their discussion.
   D. Present the problem-solving process; discuss how each step in the process occurred during the meeting.
   E. Ask what problems occurred in the process of the meeting (disagreement, apathy, hostility, etc.), and describe how they might have been handled.

VII. Conclusion
   A. Review everything covered in the session.
   B. Answer any questions.
   C. Announce future events and expectations.

   Training in problem-solving techniques should be done largely by the QC group leader. However, if assistance is needed from the Facilitator, he or she should present the needed information. Learning problem-solving techniques works best when those techniques are being applied to real problems. For that reason, participants should be asked to read their manuals prior to the start of the circle meetings, and then should apply this knowledge and develop their skills as they identify and grapple with real work-related problems.

As we have seen, effective training is an important element of the Quality Circles process. By implementing these programs carefully, and then following them up with coaching where needed, you will greatly enhance the program's chances for success.

Coaching

As process facilitator and observer, the Quality Circle Facilitator will sometimes need to act as counselor or coach to a Circle member/Circle leader. When acting as coach, the Facilitator's duty is again to help the member or leader understand and contribute to the Circle's activity so the Circle becomes a more effective problem-solving group.

In a coaching relationship, there exists the danger of the Facilitator becoming paternalistic toward the person being coached. Paternalistic behavior must be avoided because it is at odds with the participative mode of operation. The objective of Circle activity processing and coaching is to help Circle member or Circle leader learn to contribute to the Circle's activity. So, in a coaching situation, the Facilitator must help the Circle member/leader voice his/her observations, opinions, reactions and possible future responses to the Circle's activities.

To be an effective counselor, the Facilitator must remember the following guidelines to obtain the greatest results from the helper/receiver relationship:

1. **Don't argue.** The member or leader may try to preserve his self-concept by meeting your suggestions or arguments with resistance. If you increase your argumentative position or continue to "pound away" at him, you will achieve even more resistance and denial.

2. **Be prepared to listen.** You must understand the leader or member's point of view before you can begin to explore alternatives. Understanding a person's point of view, however, does not mean that you must agree with or support his position. There's a difference between empathy and sympathy.

   Let the person do most of the talking. It may be easy for you, because of your experience as a teacher, to get trapped in a prescribing or lecturing role. But a "know it all" position may threaten the person so much that he mentally leaves the scene or acts more defensively than he would if you were more receptive.

3. **Direct your comments to behavior that the member can change.** By giving people unfavorable feedback about actions over which they have little or no control, you only increase their feelings of frustration and their need to defend themselves.

4. **Give timely feedback.** Feedback is most helpful to a person when it is given at the earliest opportunity after an event or interaction has occurred. In addition, keep in mind that people may have a certain tolerance level for accepting unfavorable feedback. When this level is approached or surpassed, no further learning takes place. For this reason, you should give feedback often and in small quantities. Small change effected over a period of time will be better for the member and better for the Circle.

5. **Look at members as people,** not objects that make up your Circle headcount. They are human beings with feelings, needs, and values of their own. Try to see the world from their point of view.

6. **Reflect the feelings of the other person.** If you can focus on reflecting back the feelings and attitudes of the person instead of giving advice, he or she will be better able to find his or her own solution. When the Facilitator bounces back the feelings that the member gives off, the member can continue to talk about them. Frequent use of 'Uhn-huhn," "I see," and, "Is that so?" will help bounce the conversation back and give the subordinate a chance to elaborate.

Hints for Using Chalkboards or Flip-Pads

To add a professional touch to your session, you should become skilled at using flip-pads and blackboards during the presentation. Generally, you will be more effective if you follow the rules listed below.

1. Know in advance what words or drawings you plan to use. This helps to assure quick, confident use of the blackboard or flip-pad.

2. Write only words or phrases; avoid complete sentences. Single ideas are easier to grasp, and long sentences simply take too long to write.

3. Print. It's easier to read.

4. Use numbers to enumerate points. It helps the participants take notes.

5. Talk to the participants, not the chalkboard or flip-pad. If you must turn away from the audience, stop talking while you write. Turn back to them, and then resume talking.

6. Dress up the board with symbols, circles, arrows, boxes, underlining, quotation marks, and so on. They add some visual interest to the words.

7. Use colored chalks or marking pens if possible.

8. Do not spend long periods of time at the board. Move around. Change your pace.

9. When you have finished with the material on the board or pad, erase it, or flip to the next blank page. If people are taking notes, however, be sure they have done so before erasing or turning the material over.

10. Do not stand in front of the board or flip-pad while talking. After writing, move out of the way so people can see what you have written.

By following these rules, you will have a far more professional impact upon the participants, and your chalkboard or flip-pad will add significantly to their learning and understanding of the material.

Hints on Getting and Handling Audience Participation

The people who attend this session almost certainly will find the material interesting, for it will relate directly to their lives and roles as supervisors and managers. However, in order for learning and understanding truly to occur, it is important that they be invited to participate in the session, certainly as questioners and discussants, and perhaps as role players and analysts. To help you involve participants in the session, we suggest the things listed below:

Getting Participation

We know that audience participation is desirable and that the way people learn is by taking an active part in the situation. But how do you get participation in the first place? The most commonly used device is the "nondirected question," where you ask some question of the entire audience. The question, "Are there any questions?" is a common and usually ineffective example of the nondirected question. But such questions can also be more specific, asking the audience to react to some particular point made during the session. For example: "Did all of you understand the part about using check sheets to construct Pareto diagrams?" or "What things should you say to employees concerning conflict?" Questions like these are directed to the entire group, so that no one person has responsibility to give an answer. For that reason, this type of question often is not a good way of stimulating participation. Still, it may be the first type of question you ask when trying to get audience participation.

When nondirected questions do not provoke participation, directed questions are more effective. As their name implies, they are directed toward a specific member of the audience. By asking a particular individual his or her thoughts or ideas concerning a point in the presentation, you may be able to stimulate the thinking and participation of many audience members. This strategy is particularly effective in encouraging listeners who are shy or reluctant to ask questions; when communication between you as the facilitator and some member of the audience has been established, it becomes much easier for other audience members, who no longer are faced with having to "go first," to speak up.

The directed question must be used in accordance with certain rules. First, you should be almost certain that the person on whom you call has some answer. If you make someone in the audience look stupid by asking something he or she does not know, other listeners will be discouraged from participating. In fact, to be absolutely sure that you do not embarrass an audience member with a directed question, you might contact one of them prior to the meeting and tell him or her that you intend to ask him or her a particular question, and give that person a chance to think about an answer. Alternatively, if there is someone in the audience who always has something to say, or who seems to have an answer to everything, call on that person.

Second, your directed question should require more than a simple Yes or No. Your purpose, after all, is to get participation by your audience. Getting a one-word answer to a question does not constitute audience interaction.

Third, be sure to spread your directed questions around. Call on several different people, rather than just on the same two or three people each time.

Finally, use nonverbal feedback as a cue for deciding whom you will call on. If you are making some point to the audience and see someone openly shaking his or her head "No," or even nodding his or her head "Yes," you might call on that person to explain why he or she agrees or disagrees. Obviously, you know they have some feelings about the point; after all, they were reacting fairly strongly to it. Their expressing their feelings openly may involve others in the following discussion.

A final device for promoting participation is the "redirected question." In using this device, you simply redirect a question to the person who asked it or to another member of the audience. Thus, you might respond to a question by saying, "That's an excellent question, and I suspect you have given it some thought yourself. What do you think the answer is?" Or "Bill, you've had some experience in that area. How would you answer Fred's question?" Or, "I think that question concerns all of us. Does anyone have an answer?" In effect, rather than providing an immediate answer to the question, you direct it back to the questioner, to some other individual in the audience, or to the audience as a whole. All of these produce far more participation than does simply giving the answer yourself.

Handling audience participation

There are a number of principles you should keep in mind when handling participation by audience members. These include:

- Do not allow one or two people to dominate the meeting. Give everyone a chance to talk by calling on the quiet people and encouraging the long-winded people to keep their contributions short.

- Give answers everyone can understand. If you have to use an unusual term or expression that people in the audience might not understand, explain the term or give needed background. Be sure everyone knows what you are talking about, even though only one person asked the question.

- When answering question, speak to all audience members. Do not just look at the person who asked the question.

- Respond encouragingly to all questions. Even if the question is strange, makes no sense, or is just plain "dumb," react in a way that will make others want to ask questions. If you say, "Are there any other stupid questions," people will not be likely to ask whatever happens to be on their minds.

- If the audience is large and the question is asked by someone in front, repeat the question so everyone can hear what it was.

- Avoid confrontations. Occasionally, you may have someone in the audience who wants to argue with you, provoke you, and so on. At all costs, avoid becoming involved in an argument or confrontation. Offer to talk with the person after the meeting; change the topic; call on someone else. Do whatever is necessary to avoid an open conflict. Disagreement is fine, of course. Protracted arguments, however, simply kill the meeting.

To generate participation during the session, then, you need both to stimulate the thinking and interest of the participants and to provide them with the opportunity to talk once they have been stimulated. Asking non-directed questions can provide the opportunity; asking directed questions and redirecting questions can also stimulate thinking and interest. Controlling and encouraging participation, finally, serve to maintain participation once it develops. The more practiced and skilled you become in these communication skills, the more effective your sessions will be.

5

Circle Building

When the circle leaders and participants have been trained in effective leadership, communication, and problem-solving skills, they will be ready to move into the Quality Circle process and begin analyzing and solving problems. However, at that point they may encounter yet another new situation — one of group interaction and participative decision-making. In spite of the orientation and training given these people, and in spite of the many meetings they may have attended together as a part of their everyday work activities, these people still may have difficulty adjusting to the new environment which Quality Circles meetings create. In this chapter, then, we will consider how you, acting as facilitator, might help them in their adjustment period. Just as you helped these people to build their skills in the previous chapter, so now will you help them to build an effective group relationship.

Observation of Quality Circles groups in action has shown that they progress in certain predictable ways, and that they encounter certain predictable problems. In the following sections, we will study those developmental and problem stages, and look for ways in which you can ease them through each.

Stages of Group Development

Bringing people together in a group and calling the group a Quality Circle by no means guarantees that the group will achieve positive results. A circle's productivity will depend directly upon the degree to which it becomes an effectively operating team.

Moreover, even an effectively operating team cannot be expected to be without problems throughout its existence. It is normal for a Quality Circle to go through predictable stages during its operational life, and during stages of lowered effectiveness it will take the cooperative efforts of the Circle leader and the Facilitator to revitalize the circle and bring it back to its highest potential for productivity.

It is therefore important that you have an understanding of these developmental stages that occur during the existence of a Quality Circle, and to sense when revitalizing action by the Leader and the Facilitator is required. We will give examples of regenerating actions, but revitalization will best be achieved by specific "on-the-scene" observations and the creativity of both the Leader and Facilitator.

Stage 1 — Introduction

The first stage is an introductory phase during which the Quality Circle is initially formed. The workers will have received an indoctrination to Quality Circles by the Facilitator and will have voluntarily agreed to start a circle in their particular work area. All that can be said at this point is that each new Quality Circle formed constitutes the beginning of a prospectively dynamic problem solving team. To a great extent much of what the circle becomes will depend upon the guidance and support they receive from the Leader and Facilitator. These key people have a great responsibility for tapping the human resources existing in each circle and developing it to the fullest.

Stage 2 — Dependence

The second stage — the period during which members are instructed in Quality Circle techniques and policies — is one of dependence. Circle members do not know what is expected of them and they are dependent on their Leader and Facilitator for training and direction. The members possess no real authority during this stage. It is crucial that during this training stage the members receive a solid schooling in the problem solving techniques which will become the backbone of their Quality Circle.

Stage 3 — Counter Dependence

Following this period of almost total dependence there can come a stage of counter-dependence during which authority issues begin to emerge, and conflicts arise. Circle members now have a better grasp of the program, and may feel moved to challenge program policies and techniques. For example, it is not uncommon for members to object to the length of the training phase. Impatience develops and members want to rush into problem solving before they understand the fundamental techniques. Rebellion against the Leader, and management in general, may also emerge at this time. In spite of the Leader's instructions that they concentrate initially on the problems in their own area, circles often want to place blame on other departments or upon a management policy. It is imperative at this point for the Circle Leader and Facilitator to be assertive in adhering to the guidelines of the Quality Circle Program.

Stage 4 — Resolution of Authority

For a successful circle there will be an amiable resolution of the authority issue, and the circle will enter into a stage where members understand that they must work as a disciplined team in conjunction with the Leader. Traditionally defined roles such as "supervisor" versus "employee" are minimized, and an equality of status emerges as Leader and members work together as teammates.

State 5 — Enchantment

A stage of excitement and enchantment will normally occur at this point. Training has been completed and energies run high. Members delight in their new voice in decision making. They are proud of their contributions and the opportunity to demonstrate their abilities. Ideas flow freely and a feeling that no problem will be left unresolved prevails. Improved rapport among circle members is characteristic of this stage, and increased productivity can be expected.

Stage 6 — Disenchantment

A natural successor to this stage of enchantment is a stage of disenchantment. Members discover that not all problems can be resolved, and for those that can, implementing change can be a frustrating and difficult task. In addition, suggested solutions may be rejected and modified by management, causing members to become discouraged that their efforts were in vain. In time, the novelty of problem solving wears off and what once was a challenge now becomes a chore. Individual members in this stage tend to leave the circle or engage in non-productive behavior which negatively affects the group. Circles in this stage may unnecessarily choose to disband. It is during this stage the Facilitators and Leaders must exert extra efforts and exercise creativity to guide the circle successfully through this difficult period. It is sometimes recommended that workshops in team building and/or effective communication skills be offered to the circle at this time so that members can become aware of their own contributions to their current situation. Efforts must be exerted to direct the circle towards achieving a small success so members can once again feel encouraged to go on with their problem solving. It may be appropriate, or necessary, to invite a member of upper management to visit a circle meeting to demonstrate support of the Quality Circle concept and to show appreciation for the contributions the circle has made. Providing a measure of recognition to circle members is another suggestion. Pictures can be taken and posted on bulletin boards, or in-house newsletters published focusing on circle activities.

There is no one right answer for circles in this stage. Each situation will be unique and the corrective action will have to be tailored to suit each particular circle and situation.

Stage 7 — Interdependence

If disenchantment can be worked through, a new phase of interdependence emerges. Members now view the program more realistically and accept the fact that some of their solutions may not be accepted. They are still faced with problems in their work area which need attention and they are willing to direct their energies towards solving them. In this stage the circle redefines its approach and attitudes and decides to carry on despite the occasional roadblocks and disappointments. This is a more established period than the enchantment phase, and members will begin to engage in prime functioning during their approach to problem solving.

Stage 8 — Closure

Ultimately, all circles must prepare for closure, either because most area problems have been addressed or the circle has simply failed to jell as an effective team. At this point interest wanes, attendance falls off, and realistically everyone recognizes that the circle has served its purpose or has reached a non-productive state. It is important that the Leader and Facilitator sense this eventuality in its initial stages and begin to prepare for the dissolution of the circle. Another measure, short of final closure, which might be tried here is placing the circle in a holding or maintenance mode; scheduling meetings monthly rather than weekly until it is finally determined whether or not a circle can become productive. But once it is obvious that the circle is not productive, closure should be performed decisively and in a timely fashion.

Stage 9 — Discorporation

Thus, the final stage in the life cycle of a circle is its official discorporation. It is recommended that management attend to express appreciation to the circle for their involvement and assistance. Recognition should be given to every circle member during this meeting.

It should be noted that while these stages are normal behavior for all circles, the sequential pattern may vary from circle to circle, with any given circle fluctuating from one phase to another at any time. In addition, an individual member may be in a different phase than the circle as a whole. However, an understanding of the normal stages and probable progression can help Leaders and members alike to realize what is happening to them as a circle, and to determine what must be done to operate with maximum effectiveness.

In summary, it should be noted that the long term success of a Quality Circles program is dependent upon two important factors: the dedication of the Leaders and Facilitators to the concept of participative programs, and their mutual ability to meet the operational needs of each circle as it progresses through its evolutionary stages.

Circle Building

A Quality Circle is a group of people engaged in solving a problem. As a group, they have a better chance of reaching problem solution than does any one member working alone. This is what is known as group synergy. The better the members can work together, the better are their chances of problem solution. Therefore, each Circle needs to be a group of people who can communicate openly, be trusting, and be capable of sharing with and understanding one another so they can more easily share data and reach problem resolution. The extent to which the Circle members do not feel open, cooperative and trusting with each other is the extent to which there is a need for Circle building.

Circle building is the development, through process observation, of a candid, cooperative, trusting group that supports and respects one another's individual abilities and characteristics while working together to solve a common problem. The effective group will solve problems and develop individual, as well as group, skills. Therefore, the goals of Circle building are:

1. More open communication, cooperation and trust among Circle members.
2. More effective problem solving.
3. A mutual understanding of each member's role in the Circle.
4. An understanding in common throughout the Circle of its role in the organization.
5. More cooperation among all members of the organization.
6. Increased cooperation among work groups in the organization.

Some Circles have less need for Circle building than others because those Circles have fewer stresses placed on them. The stress affecting a Circle can be either within the Circle or external to the Circle, as Table 1 shows. Because Circle building is a development of awareness of the processes within the Circle, it is easy for the Facilitator to become engrossed in the activities of the Circle and forget that external forces may also cause stress for the Circle. It is important that the Facilitator remain aware of both potential stress sources.

When stress is present in small amounts, it motivates the circle members. Conflict among personalities may bring about better critical thinking and problem solutions; unclear goals may move the members to set goals themselves. However, when most or all of the conditions listed in Table 1 are present the group will not be able to function effectively. They will be confused, frustrated, and possibly hostile toward one another, toward the leader, and eventually toward the entire program. For these reasons, then, it is important that the Facilitator determine whether these problems or stresses exist in the group at the very beginning, and that, when needed, he or she take action to relieve those stresses.

Table 2 presents some activities that can and should be used early in a group's life to deal with the stresses that may be present.

Table 1

Stress

Internal to Circle	External to Circle
1. Expectations of Circle members.	1. Expectations of other work groups, management.
2. Conflict among personalities.	2. Conflict between status quo and Circle effort.
3. No support: members consider Circle meeting time as "time off."	3. No support — employee recognition from organization.
4. Other groups: sub-grouping within Circle.	4. Other groups: competition, conflict, mistrust from other Circles, work groups.
5. Circle building — behavior of Circle members under close examination.	5. Circle building: employees outside of Circle effort become jealous.
6. Lack of skills: job skills, problem solving skills, interpersonal skills, defensiveness develops.	6. Lack of skills; less effort by organization to develop skills of employees not in Circle.
7. Misunderstanding resources: members do not know of resources that other members have.	7. Misunderstanding resources: no understanding of management investments, organizational goals; no understanding of skills and resources of other employees; interaction of departments.
8. Unclear goals: not stated, never used before.	8. Unclear goals: not stated, never used before.

Table 2

Circle Building Steps

Activity	Stress Relaxed (from Table 1)
1. Analyze stresses on Circle.	1. Note whether internal or external stresses.
2. Management committed to Quality Circle effort as employee development effort.	2. Relaxes external stresses of: — Management expectations — Support from organization. — Understanding organizational goals. — Understanding of investments.
3. Management kept informed through progress reports, distribution of minutes, presentations.	3. Relaxes external stresses of lack of support, wrong expectations, unclear goals.

Activity	Stress Relaxed (from Table 1)
4. Employee population kept informed through acknowledgement of Circle effort, with expectations of expansion, public notice of Circle progress, and actual expansion.	4. Relaxes external stresses of other work group expectations, conflict, competition, jealousy, and interaction of departments.
5. Establish Circle's objectives for Circle building.	5. Relaxes internal stresses resulting from: — Expectations of Circle members. — Conflict among personalities. — No support — members consider meeting time as "time off." — Unclear goals.
6. Circle determines expectations and resources within the Circle.	6. Reduces internal stresses of: — Conflicts among personalities. — Misunderstandings of resources. — Expectations. — Sub-grouping.
7. State goals of each Circle meeting clearly.	7. Relaxes internal stresses of: — Expectations of Circle members — Members seeing meeting time as "time off." — Unclear goals.
8. Evaluate success in goal attainment and processes involved.	8. Relaxes internal stresses of: — Expectations. — Conflict. — Sub-grouping. — Interpersonal skills. — Defensiveness. — Misunderstanding resources.
9. Deal with process problems.	9. Relaxes all internal stresses.
10. Start problem-solving activities.	10. Relaxes internal stress of: — Expectations. — Meeting seen as "time off." — Lack of problem-solving skills — Misunderstanding resources.
11. Make Circle's process an agenda item.	11. Relaxes all internal stresses.
12. Include training or other Circle development activities as needed.	12. May relax any of the internal stresses, especially lack of skill.
13. Promote Circle activities to rest of organization.	13. Relaxes both internal and external stresses resulting from expectations, support, Circle building, misunderstanding of resources, and unclear goals.

As Table 2 suggests, communications that are as candid as possible and still protect the Circle's effort at Circle building are the best mechanism for dealing with the external stresses. The Facilitator should make sure that management develops commitment to the Circle effort as an employee development effort from the start. Also, management needs to know how well the effort is progressing and then frequently receive information comparing the progress the Circle has made to the expectations which were stated at the beginning of the Circle implementation. If progress of the Circle effort is not as expected, the Facilitator needs to take the time to explain why there are differences.

The employee population that is not in Quality Circles also needs to be kept informed. At the early stages of the Circle effort, acknowledgement of the Circle effort and expectations of expansion are enough to communicate the program. Later, everyone needs to hear, in a formal way, about the solutions, changes and progress that Circles have caused in the organization. Again, promises of and actual expansion should accompany the reports. Such reporting to the employee population will do a lot to dispell feelings of mistrust, inadequacy, competition, and conflict that can be felt by the employee population not in Circles.

The Circle also must deal with internal stresses. As the Circle looks at its own process, the Facilitator should consider the stresses listed as internal stresses in Table 1. During the first Circle building meeting, the Facilitator and leader should ask the Circle to take the time to establish the objectives of Circle building. During the next couple of meetings, the Circle should (if necessary) take time to know the other Circle members better. For instance, each member might take a statement about his/her expectations of Circle meetings and the resources he/she brings to the group. Such sharing of expectations rids the group of internal stresses of false expectations and misunderstanding of Circle member resources. If these sessions are started with clear statements of what is going to happen, the Circle will learn to state goals clearly and examine their efforts to see if they have done what they stated that they would. Along the way, the Facilitator should encourage statements and behaviors that examine group conflict and use conflict to the group's advantage. Statements which include all members in Circle activity, and statements of mutual support should also be encouraged.

After the Circle has learned about their own resources and expectations, Circle building can continue during problem solving Circle meetings where the Circle begins to use problem solving techniques to work on their chosen problems. The Circle leader can ask a Circle member and the Facilitator to act as process observer, so that the Circle's process becomes an agenda item for discussion and is subject to continued improvement. As the Circle becomes better and better at dealing with the Circle's processing as well as problem solving, the Facilitator advances from process facilitator to process observer, to invited Circle guest and administrator of the Circle effort. In the latter role the Facilitator is a resource person, making sure that training and other Circle needs are met, and a promoter, making sure that the external forces do not go out of line and that the Circles are supported and positively recognized.

Common Problems in Circle Building

Working in Quality Circles can be exceptionally rewarding or extremely frustrating. A Circle which builds itself carefully and successfully is extremely exciting and enjoyable, while a Circle which does not build itself well requires much more patience. We have noted a number of common pitfalls encountered during the Circle building process, and these must be watched for and avoided.

Unrealistic Goals

Many groups attempt more than they can accomplish. Their goals may be so broad and vague that they create frustration among the members, leading to rapid disenchantment. One major aim in working with Quality Circles is to work toward specific, achievable goals. Early achievement leads to a feeling of success — the only thing that can sustain long-term effort. For this reason, Quality Circles should be strongly urged to select a major theme within which to work, and then to work on one small problem at a time. All other problem solutions mean little unless members feel that they are progressing towards an achievable goal.

Lack of Adquate Contract

One of the broadest and most basic problems facing Quality Circle groups is the lack of an adequate contract between the group and its membership. Most groups and organizations are not explicit about expectations for their members. Most groups also do not allow the members to indicate their resources, experience, and backgrounds. Hence, a specific agreement between members and the organization regarding what each person can and will do is rare. Discovering members' resources and establishing members' time commitments usually occur informally and haphazardly, costing the group much maintenance time. Under-utilization of member skills and experiences if often the result. Quality Circle Facilitators are encouraged to devote at least one meeting, early in the life of the Circle, to develop this contract.

A Circle meeting to share individual resources and Circle expectations is useful. Members are asked to respond to the following questions:

- "What resources do I bring to the Circle?"
- "What do I expect from the Circle?"

Members then introduce themselves to other members by discussing their answers.

Lack of Leadership and Accountability

Reluctance to confront the problem of leadership accountability is common in many groups. Yet failure to establish adequate leadership structures and to make members accountable for their responsibilities is a fault which seriously hampers the effectiveness of most volunteer groups. There are several ways to avoid this problem.

Project Leaders. An effort should be made to identify project leaders for each major theme attempted. If possible, this task should be assumed by one of the more active members. The project leader is responsible for seeing that the project is successfully completed. Program charts and well developed action plans will aid in getting members to accept responsibility.

Regular Staff Meetings. The Facilitator should conduct regular Quality Circle Leader meetings intended to examine progress toward objectives, to exchange information about each group, and to discuss problems. These meetings result in a sense of group cohesiveness and a climate of support.

Orientation. The more time spent on orientation, the quicker the new member becomes a working member of the Circle. An effective orientation method is the "buddy system": assigning one member to work closely with each new member, to answer questions, and generally to familiarize him with the work. The veteran member can also assist the new member in developing a Circle responsibility.

Lack of Rewards or Recognition

A major failure of volunteer organizations lies in neglecting to recognize member efforts. Quality Circle members quietly assist the organization by solving the problems and make their recommendations to management. Management must then recognize the members for their contributions even if, for good reasons, their suggestion is not implemented. In some organizations, management's recognition is the only outward reward the member receives.

Lack of Attention to Group Process

Most volunteer groups do not give adequate thought to how they work together. Decision-making methods and other group norms are not determined explicitly. Group-process activities can aid the group in becoming more effective.

One Circle member may be assigned as a process observer. The existence of this role makes Circle dynamics a legitimate discussion item. The observer points out those items that are hindering Circle effectiveness and suggests preventative actions. For example, the observer may ask the Circle to pursue the problem of how to prevent certain members from dominating meetings. The role of the process observer could revolve among members, so that all become accustomed to observing the process. A check list of process objectives could be an important aid for the observer.

Regular agenda items for meetings can sustain the Circle thinking about its process. The question might be as simple as "How are we performing as a Circle?" More complicated instruments can also be used. However it is accomplished, it is important to monitor process continuously.

Summary

In this chapter, we have considered some techniques of effective circle building. After describing the developmental stages through which most circles proceed, we suggested several types of internal and external stress which commonly inhibit circle effectiveness. Many of these sources of stress are resolved simply by implementing the skills taught in the **Quality Circles Leader's Manual** and the **Quality Circles Participant's Manual.** However, others require specific action on the part of the Facilitator. Finally, to guide the Facilitator's efforts more precisely, we suggested five specific problems common to Quality Circle groups, and indicated ways in which each of them might be resolved. By combining these circle building measures with the skill building techniques discussed in the preceding chapter, you will virtually ensure the success of the Quality Circles system.

6

Promoting, Rewarding, and Expanding the Quality Circles Process

In this manual, we have considered a number of important topics: the stages through which Quality Circles implementation should go, the ways in which management support can be obtained, the planning and process tracking techniques which should be developed, and the ways in which skills and circles should be built. All of these things were to be done either before the circles themselves began, or during initial circle meetings.

Now, however, we must look to the future. What happens once the circles are going? How do we promote the process as it occurs? How do we reward the participants and leaders for their efforts? Ultimately, how do we expand the program? These things comprise the topics to be considered in this sixth chapter.

Promoting Quality Circles

Before exploring specific techniques for promoting the Quality Circles effort, we first must sound a note of warning. When starting a program which is innovative, "state of the art," and likely to save the organization a great deal of time and money, the natural tendency is to over-promote the program — to tell the world about the wonderful thing which is about to occur. This tendency can lead to three potential problems.

First, it can arouse too much interest among supervisors and employees, making it necessary either to include a large number of people at the very beginning, or to omit a large number of people from the initial pilot project. Either can be dangerous. If everyone is included at the outset, any mistakes or flaws in the system become disasters, and anything that goes wrong affects everyone. For that reason, smaller pilot programs are almost always preferred. On the other hand, the people left out of the pilot program may be somewhat resentful, and in a few rare instances may even work to undermine the program.

Second, when a pilot program is used, a great deal of pressure from the people not in the program may be exerted to expand the program as quickly as possible. Thus, rather than waiting six months or so to be sure that the program works and the "kinks" have been ironed out, management may bow to the pressure and expand the program after only one or two months. Again, the result may be that mistakes suddenly become big mistakes, not confined only to the small pilot group.

Finally, if the community is notified of the project, or if customer groups are told that the organization is starting this wonderful new program, management will feel a great deal of pressure to make that program work. Such pressure may be beneficial in creating management interest and commitment, but it also may cause management to push too hard for immediate results. If, for some reason, the program should not live up to expectations, either in the minds of management or in the minds of the community and customers, then the organization may suffer some embarrassment as well.

The lesson, then, is this. First, start the program on a pilot basis. Probably no more than 6 to 12 circles should be started initially, and the promotional efforts at the beginning of the process should be just enough to bring these groups into being. As the program progresses, more active promotional efforts should occur. Thus, the second lesson is to promote the process when it has achieved something worth advertising. Only at that point should the internal and external communication media begin to churn out Quality Circles propaganda.

Promotional Phases

To promote is "to work actively to stir up interest for the accomplishment of something." A good portion of the facilitator's activities deal with "working actively to stir up interest" in Quality Circles.

The first act of Circle promotion for the Circle Facilitator is the activities involved in obtaining management commitment to the Quality Circle effort. As mentioned in Chapter II, the usual way of gaining management commitment is to determine the organizational needs that Quality Circles can meet, and to give a presentation to management about the benefits to the organization that can be gained from Quality Circles. The amount of "selling" that is necessary before and after the presentation varies from none to a lot in a particular organization. In some organizations, management has already formed a commitment to Quality Circles even before these presentations occur.

After management decides to implement the process, the Circle Facilitator needs to develop an orientation for the potential Circle leaders. This promotional activity should define Quality Circles, state the organization's expectations, describe the Circle leader's role and responsibilities, enumerate the intrinsic rewards for the leaders, and restate the organization's commitment to Quality Circles to reassure the supervisors. The form of the orientation session can be anything from an informal question and answer session to a slide or videotape show. Let the size of the group, other group characteristics, and expectations of the organization (including tradition and budget) determine the form of the orientation.

The next Quality Circle promotion need is creating an appropriate level of employee awareness of Quality Circles. The employees must be informed about Quality Circles, and must be convinced that it's not just "another management program." But, especially when starting with a pilot program, it is not appropriate to overstate or make too much fanfare about starting the Quality Circle effort. At the beginning, the first participants need some privacy to make the best attempts at a new way of organizational life. Creating a "fishbowl" environment through over-promotion simply makes life more difficult for them.

After signing up volunteer Circle leaders from the orientation session, the next step is Circle leader training. Besides being a training session, Circle leader training can be a potential promotional tool. If those leaders tell others in the organization that the training is a good developmental experience, the leader training can be a very positive promotional device. Similarly, favorable reactions by circle participants to the training they receive also can promote the program.

During the first few weeks of Circle activity promotion should be kept lowkey and aimed at supporting Circle building (see Chapter V). And, during the Circle building stage, the Facilitator will be kept busy dealing with the internal and external stresses to build the best environment possible for Circle building.

When the Circles have reached the problem study stage, the Facilitator will have to have all administrative paperwork in place so that the Circles can report their progress to appropriate parts of the organization. This is probably one of the most critical promotional points. The Circle must be able to report enough progress that management will recognize and support the Circle activity. The Circle must also have enough privacy so that if they hit a snag, the members will not feel foolish or frustrated and quit. The Facilitator must find organizationally acceptable ways to protect the Circle while still promoting the Circle activity in the rest of the organization.

When the circles begin to develop solutions, pose action plans, and have their plans implemented by management, the need for active promotion becomes strongest. As we have noted before, much of the reward for participating in Quality Circles is the recognition circle members receive from management, supervision, and their own peers. If that recognition is to come about, however, the achievements of each circle must be communicated loudly and frequently. It is here, then, that presentations to management, publicity to the community and outside organizations, and notices to the entire work force become important elements for promoting the program. These promotions allow the organization, management, and the Facilitator, leaders, and participants all to receive proper credit for implementing this program and making it work.

Finally, expansion of the program occurs through promotional efforts. Supervisors and employees need to be notified that the program is going to be expanded, and need to be given an opportunity to volunteer. The interest generated by the communications of circle successes should make this step relatively easy to achieve. Thus, all that may be needed is a notice to supervisors that the process is to be expanded and volunteers are needed, and then notification by those supervisors selected to their people that employee volunteers in their own areas are needed.

Overall, then, the strategy in promoting Quality Circles is to start slowly, and then gradually to build momentum as the process builds. Initially, the process should be promoted just enough to gain management commitment and obtain participation; ultimately, however, the process should be recognized for the things it has achieved and changes it has created.

Promotional Techniques

There are a number of methods that can be used to promote Quality Circles. These include:

Formal Presentations. We have mentioned these several times. Formal presentations are often used to orient management, supervisors, and employees to the process, and to keep management informed of circle activities. Year-end reports to management, usually given by the Facilitator, also are provided through this medium, telling management about the achievements made by the entire program.

The House Newsletter. Most organizations have a regularly-published employee newsletter. This should be used to announce the initiation of the program, to report ongoing circle activities, and above all, to recognize circle participants. A regular "Quality Circle Events" column appearing in each issue serves these purposes well, and pictures of QC groups are an effective means of rewarding those individuals.

Bulletin Boards. Bulletin board announcements and pictures are also useful for informing everyone of current circle events, and for providing recognition to participants.

Employee Handbook. Once Quality Circles are fully implemented and a permanent part of the organization, they should be discussed as a part of the organization's employee handbook. They are, after all, an important part of the organization's overall communications program, and they also are visible evidence that management is interested in employee input and willing to invest in employee development.

New Employee Orientation. Again, when the process has become a permanent fixture in the organization, those organizations having formal new employee orientation programs should incorporate Quality Circles as a part of the presentation. New employees need to be told about the program, about its role in the organization, and about any requirements they may have to meet in order to participate (such as completing the probationary period).

Special Letters. When major events occur, such as implementation of the program or later expansion of the system, employees may be notified through a special letter sent by someone in management — usually the Chief Executive Officer. This letter may be sent directly to employees' homes, distributed by the supervisors, enclosed in paycheck envelopes, or distributed through some other means. In any case, the purpose of the letter is to inform employees of the activities about to take place, and to invite their participation if appropriate.

Quality Circle Activity Reports or Newsletters. Often, an organization will develop a special activity report to be used in keeping management informed about current circle events. The forms presented in Chapter III can be used toward this end, or a special summary report or newsletter may be developed. These items should be distributed at least on a monthly basis, and perhaps more often if needed. Their purpose, of course, should be to keep management informed, but they also should maintain management support of the program.

Recruiting Materials. Quality Circles repeatedly has been found an effective recruiting tool, for potential employees often want to work in an organization where their voices will be heard and their ideas implemented. Thus, written materials used for recruiting (such as brochures or newspaper advertisements) may include a brief description of the program and a statement concerning the active involvement of employees in the analysis and design of their own work. Similarly, recruiting speeches or interviews should also present the program as a part of a description of the workplace.

Press Releases. Local newspapers should be informed of the program and the progress it is achieving once the pilot program is in place and functioning. Reporters may be invited to interview circle leaders or participants, and newspaper pictures of circle activities may be appropriate.

Community Speeches. In many communities, interest in an organization's new Quality Circles program is likely to be high. Speeches to community groups about the program and its accomplishments may therefore be an effective (and popular) means of promoting not only the program itself, but the organization as a whole.

Professional or Trade Association Articles. Nationally, interest is high in productivity improvement in general, and in Quality Circles specifically. By writing your circle experiences into an article, and submitting that article to an appropriate professional group or trade association, attention again can be drawn both to the program and to the process.

Conventions and Conferences. Just as professional and trade associations are interested in publishing Quality Circle-related articles, so too are they interested in having speeches about QC experiences given in programs at their conventions and conferences. Again, these speeches create interest in the organization and the process, and they provide some recognition to the speaker as well.

Visits by V.I.P.s. Often, local, state, or even national dignitaries are willing (even eager) to visit the organization and survey Quality Circle activities. A mayor, congressman, state senator, and so on stands to gain press coverage for himself or herself by making such a visit, and the organization and circle members also gain recognition by having the V.I.P. pay them a visit. Letters sent to these people describing the program and inviting them to visit usually are sufficient to prompt this sort of promotional activity.

Advertising. Quality Circles ultimately improve the quality of service or product offered by the organization. Thus, it is perfectly appropriate for the marketing efforts of the organization to use Quality Circles as a part of its sales effort. After all, employee involvement not only benefits the organization, it also benefits those individuals and organizations whom this organization serves. The marketing function therefore needs to let those groups know that the benefits are available.

Doubtless there are other techniques that can be used to promote Quality Circles. However, the list above suggests some methods which can be used as soon as the process is implemented, and others which can be planned for while the circles get under way. By using virtually all of these things, you can be assured of getting the maximum public relations benefit for the investment made in the QC program.

Rewarding Quality Circles

Throughout this section, we have noted that recognition needs to be extended to those who participate in the Quality Circles program. Now, however, we will become more specific about the forms which such recognition might take.

Public Recognition

The techniques for promoting Quality Circles listed above serve another important function: providing recognition to those who participate. Each of these things cause the leaders and participants to feel "special," and thus provides them with important psychological rewards.

Management Response

While the experience of presenting a recommended plan of action to top management is itself rewarding, even more rewarding is to have management accept the proposal and undertake its implementation. It is important, then, that management implement employee recommendations whenever possible, and that they go out of their way to thank employees for their efforts. Personal letters written by top-level managers to individual leaders and participants (copies of which are placed in their permanent files) often serve as useful reinforcement to the public thanks given circle members. Lastly, if the management team cannot or chooses not to implement an employee recommendation, they must take even greater care to thank employees for their efforts, to encourage them to continue working, and to inform them completely about why the recommendations cannot be put into effect. If possible, they also should suggest alternative courses of action for the group, such as other directions in which the problem might be taken or a solution developed. Again, encouraging continuing effort is important, particularly when the manner to the employees' suggestion is "no."

Performance Appraisal

Information about leader and individual participant performance should be kept regularly, perhaps using some of the techniques described in Chapter III. In turn, this information should be used as a part of the regular performance appraisal system.

Two types of performance appraisal systems might be considered. If the organization uses some variation of "management by objectives," the Quality Circle activities should themselves be made one or more of the supervisor's or employee's objectives, and should be treated in the same fashion as are other objectives. In this case, then, Quality Circles represent activities which are added to those already taken into consideration in performance appraisal. On the other hand, if a standard set of criteria (such as "quality of work," "quantity of work," "knowledge of work," and so on) are used for everyone in that job category, and then individuals are rated or ranked according to those criteria, performance in Quality Circles activities should be used as a part of those overall judgments. In other words, no criteria are added to the system; Quality Circles activities are simply considered to be another element of the person's job, and he or she is evaluated in that situation just as he or she is in all other settings. Thus, "quality of work" would consider the employee's work quality both in and out of circle meetings, as would "quantity of work," and so on.

One final point should be made here, however. Employees and supervisors who participate in Quality Circles should not be given preferential treatment in performance appraisals over those who do not. To do so would be unfair to those who wished to participate but who were not among those selected, and to those who felt for whatever reason that they would rather not take part in these activities. The same standards of performance should be applied to everyone (with the exception of performance objectives devoted specifically to circle's activities). Note, however, that if Quality Circles causes a supervisor's department to run more efficiently than some other supervisor's department, that efficiency should be rewarded, regardless of the reason it came about. Similarly, if an employee becomes so involved in QC activities that he or she neglects daily work, appraisal of that work must reflect the decrease in performance. In sum, then, you are evaluating outcomes: efficiency, quality, and so on. Those outcomes must be judged in the same way for everyone. Whether or not those outcomes are attributable to Quality Circles is, from an appraisal perspective, irrelevant.

Quality Circles and Suggestion Systems

Of major concern to many organizations contemplating the start of a Quality Circle program is the effect it will have upon their existing employee suggestion system. The answer is not easily provided. In fact, this is a question which can be answered only with regard to each specific case. We will, however, try to give some general concepts that may be adapted to specific situations.

A suggestion program offering little or no monetary reward poses little problem. Unfortunately, the converse may also be true. How can Quality Circles offering no monetary rewards compete effectively with a "paying" suggestion system for the ideas of eligible employees? Even in cases of a "non-paying" suggestion system, moreover, Quality Circles may be viewed as a threat to the vested interests of those who maintain the system.

a. The "Non-Paying" System

This concern is perhaps the easiest to resolve. The simplest solution, of course, is to funnel all Quality Circle suggestions through the established suggestion system along with whatever other suggestions are submitted from non-member employees. The caution here is the same for all Quality Circle activities. Do not allow "the system" to thwart your Quality Circles by operating so slowly on Quality Circle suggestions that the members become disenchanted with Quality Circles as just another ineffective bottle neck.

b. The "Paying" System

In the case of a "paying" system, the answer becomes complex. One method is to inaugurate the Quality Circle program on a strict non-paying basis, with little or no interface with the existing "paying" suggestion system. A number of significant suggestions will come from the Quality Circles and be implemented, perhaps with no complaint from anyone. How long it will be before the Circle members "wise-up" is unknown, however, and there may be a point at which non-monetary recognition is insufficient to sustain such an approach.

If you decide to move away from the non-monetary approach to Quality Circle rewards, the variations are legion. In some organizations a Quality Circle suggestion is accorded the same award as a suggestion from a non-Circle employee. In those cases every member of the Circle shares equally, or the award is made to the Quality Circle organization, and every member of every Circle shares equally. Some Circle awards are paid to the employee recreation program, and some are paid to a charity chosen by the Circle.

Regardless of what approach is finally adopted, a number of additional questions must be answered, such as:

- How do you determine who has earned the award in an instance where an individual and a Circle have made the same suggestion?

- When a Circle has received outside help in solving a problem, should the award be shared with the "outside helpers" and on what basis? Time spent or value of help?
- Should members who joined the Circle after the problem was being worked on or even after it had been solved share in the award, and to what degree?
- What about those members who worked on the problem for a time and dropped out of the Circle or were transferred?
- Some organizations do not allow supervisors and managers to share in awards. Should the same hold true for Circle Leaders? What if the Leader is not a supervisor?

There are certainly more questions to be answered. What we have tried to do is make you aware that the "non-pay" approach is not without it's drawbacks, but it seems much less complex than the "pay" approach. Whatever your decision, do not make it lightly, and above all, plan your system well.

Expanding Quality Circles

Assuming all goes well, you eventually will want to expand the system beyond the pilot project size, and include new employees and new areas of the organization. To achieve that expansion, you first will have to achieve four conditions:

- Management Understanding and Support. There must be enough understanding that management sees the program as helping them to achieve their goals. They need to offer enthusiastic encouragement to first-level supervisors and employees, and to provide needed resources if expansion is to proceed.
- Demonstrated Benefit. Clear evidence must be provided that the program has produced measurable results.
- Communicability. The theory and practice involved in the program must be straight forward and easy for everyone to understand.
- Expertise among Facilitators. Those charged with overseeing the expansion — the Facilitators — must have developed the expertise to initiate that process: training, monitoring, and so on.

When these conditions exist, and when you are ready to begin program expansion, here are some things to consider:

1. Coordinating Structure.

As the program grows, particularly within a large organization, the need for a coordinating structure and a single focal point increases. The Steering Committee takes on even greater importance for program planning and overall support, but there may be a need to ease the load on them by creating lower-level coordinating committees. Comprised of middle-level managers, these committees act as mini-Steering Committees, providing direction for those groups under their purview. As a general rule of thumb, for each ten or so Quality Circles, there may be a need to provide a mini-Steering Committee. More important than the number, however, is the operational function from which the circles come. A mini-committee could handle 15 circles from the same functional area — manufacturing, for example — with roughly the same amount of effort needed to oversee 8 circles from different areas — Marketing, Quality Control, Purchasing, Maintenance, and Buildings and Grounds, for example. Thus, circles should be grouped by function as much as possible, and then placed under mini-Steering Committees. The Facilitators then would have the responsibility for keeping these mini-committees coordinated with one another.

2. Available Facilitators

As the program grows, so does the need for skilled Facilitators. If too few Facilitators were trained at the beginning of the pilot program, those people (perhaps with the assistance of a consultant) will need to train the new Facilitators. As before, these Facilitators will be needed to train new circle leaders and participants, and to oversee early circle meetings.

3. Expansion Strategies

There are a number of ways in which the decision can be made whether or not to expand the program into certain areas. The program can remain entirely voluntary, or management may decide to request participation by certain supervisors and employees. While the pilot project may have deliberately avoided troublesome departments or units in the organization, an expanded program may deliberately draw those departments in. After all, Quality Circles is now a proven process in this organization, and it can be used to involve and improve departments where it is most needed. Moreover, the successful track record of the program will place a little bit of added pressure upon the new supervisor. Their peers have made it work in the past, so it is reasonable to expect them to make it work now. Finally, an employee opinion survey conducted to assess the effects of the pilot program also may point the way for program expansion. A number of departments or groups may loudly request participation in the program, or some specific problems may emerge on the survey which can be solved by implementation of Quality Circles.

4. Expansion Stages

A few organizations have succumbed to the temptation to over-expand their program. After finding the pilot plan successful, they involved virtually everyone in the organization in the expanded plan, and then found the whole thing unmanageable. To avoid this difficulty, expansion must be slow and incremental. Approximately 6 months after the pilot groups started (assuming things are going well), additional groups might be trained and formed. Probably not more than 10 to 12 groups should be added at this point. Three months later, another 10 to 12 groups might be added. And so the process would go, a few groups being added every three or four months. This sort of incremental process gives the organization a chance to adjust gradually to the process, and provides the facilitator an opportunity to develop coordinating and record-keeping mechanisms as the need arises. Above all, if the system starts to become unmanageable, expansion beyond the current number can be halted, and the current groups can be brought under control.

Summary

In this final chapter, we have looked beyond the initial training and implementation stages and considered ways of promoting, rewarding, and expanding successful Quality Circles programs. It is here, really, that the work involved in setting up and starting Quality Circles begins to pay off for everyone involved. Social rewards, public recognition, and even financial reward and professional advancement all can be tied to participation in Quality Circles, so that the benefits reaped by the organization are shared by the individuals who brought those benefits about. These are the things to look toward as you work to bring Quality Circles to life.

Sample Overhead Transparencies

QUALITY CIRCLES ARE:

GROUPS OF EMPLOYEES . . . . .

FROM THE SAME DEPARTMENT OR WORK GROUP . . . . .

WHO MEET REGULARLY . . . . .

TO IDENTIFY, ANALYZE, AND SOLVE WORK-RELATED PROBLEMS

COMMON QUALITY CIRCLE OBJECTIVES INCLUDE:

- IMPROVING QUALITY OF SERVICE OR PRODUCTS

- REDUCING WORK-RELATED ERRORS

- PROMOTING COST REDUCTION

- DEVELOPING IMPROVED TEAMWORK

- DEVELOPING IMPROVED WORK METHODS

- IMPROVING EFFICIENCY

- IMPROVING MANAGEMENT-EMPLOYEE RELATIONS

- PROMOTING LEADERSHIP DEVELOPMENT

- PROMOTING CAREER DEVELOPMENT

- IMPROVING COMMUNICATION HOUSE-WIDE

- INCREASING AWARENESS OF SAFETY

- REDUCING TURNOVER

- IMPROVING PUBLIC RELATIONS

116

ADVANTAGES OF QUALITY CIRCLES

- Improves quality & cost awareness.
- Requires little or no change in organizational structure.
- Educational & work oriented.
- Rewards are in the work itself.
- Flexible, adaptable to any organization.
- Improves communications.
- Reduces conflicts.
- Links all levels & functions of the organization.

117

HISTORICAL DEVELOPMENT OF QUALITY CIRCLES

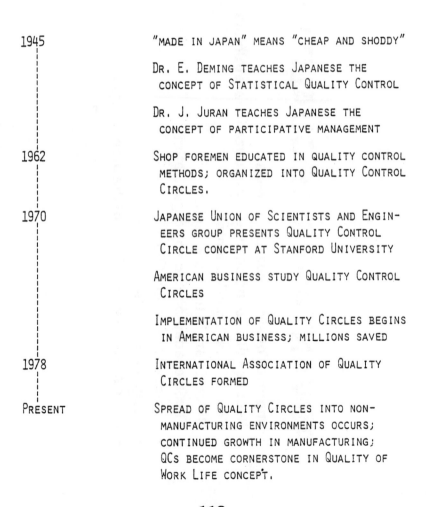

1945   "MADE IN JAPAN" MEANS "CHEAP AND SHODDY"

                    DR. E. DEMING TEACHES JAPANESE THE
                    CONCEPT OF STATISTICAL QUALITY CONTROL

                    DR. J. JURAN TEACHES JAPANESE THE
                    CONCEPT OF PARTICIPATIVE MANAGEMENT

1962   SHOP FOREMEN EDUCATED IN QUALITY CONTROL
                    METHODS; ORGANIZED INTO QUALITY CONTROL
                    CIRCLES.

1970   JAPANESE UNION OF SCIENTISTS AND ENGIN-
                    EERS GROUP PRESENTS QUALITY CONTROL
                    CIRCLE CONCEPT AT STANFORD UNIVERSITY

                    AMERICAN BUSINESS STUDY QUALITY CONTROL
                    CIRCLES

                    IMPLEMENTATION OF QUALITY CIRCLES BEGINS
                    IN AMERICAN BUSINESS; MILLIONS SAVED

1978   INTERNATIONAL ASSOCIATION OF QUALITY
                    CIRCLES FORMED

PRESENT   SPREAD OF QUALITY CIRCLES INTO NON-
                    MANUFACTURING ENVIRONMENTS OCCURS;
                    CONTINUED GROWTH IN MANUFACTURING;
                    QCS BECOME CORNERSTONE IN QUALITY OF
                    WORK LIFE CONCEPT.

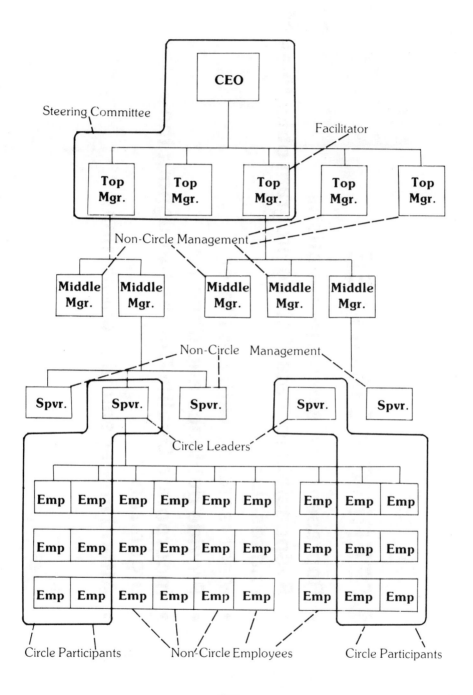

STEERING COMMITTEE

- Representatives of major functions
- Responsible for establishing program objectives and resources
- Meet regularly with facilitator
- Provide guidance and direction
- Incorporate Quality Circles throughout the organization
- Attend management presentations

120

QUALITY CIRCLE FACILITATOR

- Responsible for Quality Circle program operation
- Works closely with Steering Committee
- Trains members & Leaders
- Coordinates Circle operations
- Interfaces between Circles & other organizations
- Maintains records

121

Quality Circle Leader

- Current organizational supervisor
- Responsible for operation of Circle
- Works closely with Facilitator
- Attends leadership training
- Teaches Circle members
- Participates in Leader Circle

IMPLEMENTING QUALITY CIRCLES

PHASE I: PROGRAM INITIATION

  A. "DISCOVERY" OF QUALITY CIRCLES
  B. DEVELOPING INITIAL SUPPORT
  C. SETTING PRELIMINARY OBJECTIVES
  D. BUILDING MANAGEMENT SUPPORT
  E. DECIDING TO START

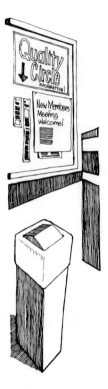

PHASE II: PROGRAM STRUCTURING

  F. ORGANIZING STEERING COMMITTEE
  G. SELECTING FACILITATOR(S)
  H. FINALIZING OBJECTIVES
  I. DEVELOPING IMPLEMENTATION PLAN
  J. COLLECTING BASE-LINE DATA
  K. BRIEFING MANAGEMENT
  L. SELECTING CIRCLE LEADERS
  M. PUBLICIZING PROGRAM

PHASE III: SKILLS DEVELOPMENT

  N. FACILITATOR TRAINING
  O. LEADER TRAINING
  P. PARTICIPANT TRAINING: CLASSROOM
  Q. PARTICIPANT TRAINING: CIRCLE ACTIVITIES

PHASE IV: PROGRAM IMPLEMENTATION

  R. PROBLEMS AND CAUSES IDENTIFIED
  S. SOLUTIONS & ACTION PLANS DEVELOPED
  T. PRESENTATIONS TO MIDDLE AND TOP MGT. MADE
  U. CHANGES IMPLEMENTED & COMMUNICATED
  V. CIRCLES RECOGNIZED

PHASE V. PROGRAM REVIEW AND EXPANSION

123

PARTICIPANT TRAINING INCLUDES:

CLASSROOM TRAINING BY FACILITATOR IN
EFFECTIVE COMMUNICATION TECHNIQUES, SUCH AS:

- LISTENING SKILLS
- AVOIDING VERBAL BARRIERS
- PERCEIVING PEOPLE ACCURATELY
- USING NONVERBAL COMMUNICATION
- ADAPTING TO THE GROUP ENVIRONMENT
- USING GROUP PROCESSES
- WORKING TOWARD GROUP CONSENSUS
- UNDERSTANDING HUMAN MOTIVATION
- OVERCOMING APATHY, HOSTILITY, AND DEFENSIVENESS

CIRCLE TRAINING BY CIRCLE LEADER IN
EFFECTIVE PROBLEM-SOLVING TECHNIQUES, SUCH AS:

- ANALYZING WORK
- IDENTIFYING PROBLEMS
- GATHERING AND DISPLAYING INFORMATION
- PRIORITIZING PROBLEMS
- BRAINSTORMING
- MAKING DECISIONS
- EVALUATING ALTERNATIVES
- DEVELOPING ACTION PLANS

CLASSROOM AND CIRCLE TRAINING BY EXPERT TRAINER IN
EFFECTIVE PRESENTATION TECHNIQUES

CIRCLE LEADER TRAINING INCLUDES:

TRAINING IN ALL TOPICS TAUGHT CIRCLE PARTICIPANTS, PLUS:

CLASSROOM TRAINING BY FACILITATOR IN
EFFECTIVE GROUP LEADERSHIP TECHNIQUES, SUCH AS:

- EVALUATING THEIR MANAGEMENT STYLE
- IMPLEMENTING PARTICIPATIVE MANAGEMENT
- CONDUCTING EFFECTIVE MEETINGS
- EVALUATING MEETINGS
- EVALUATING EMPLOYEE CONTRIBUTIONS IN MEETINGS
- TEACHING PARTICIPANTS PROBLEM-SOLVING METHODS

CLASSROOM TRAINING BY EXPERT IN
EFFECTIVE PRESENTATION TECHNIQUES AND
TECHNIQUES FOR MODERATING GROUP PRESENTATIONS

FACILITATOR TRAINING INCLUDES:

TRAINING IN ALL TOPICS TAUGHT CIRCLE PARTICIPANTS, PLUS

TRAINING IN ALL TOPICS TAUGHT CIRCLE LEADERS, PLUS:

INDIVIDUAL OR SEMINAR INSTRUCTION BY CONSULTANT IN
QUALITY CIRCLES SYSTEMS, SUCH AS:

- STRUCTURING THE QUALITY CIRCLES PROGRAM
- INVOLVING MANAGEMENT AT ALL LEVELS
- IDENTIFYING AND RESOLVING POTENTIAL PROBLEMS
- "SELLING" THE CIRCLES PROGRAM
- SCHEDULING AND COORDINATING CIRCLES ACTIVITIES
- EVALUATING CIRCLE PARTICIPANTS AND LEADERS
- TEACHING CIRCLE LEADERS
- TEACHING CIRCLE PARTICIPANTS
- EXPANDING THE QUALITY CIRCLES PROGRAM

INDIVIDUAL COACHING AND MONITORING BY CONSULTANT
DURING INITIAL PHASES OF IMPLEMENTATION AND
LEADER AND PARTICIPANT TRAINING

POTENTIAL PROBLEMS

- Existing suggestion program
- Labor union relationship
- Failure of previous programs
- Poor management response to suggestions
- Impatience
- Selecting problems too difficult for Circle
- Scheduling problems
- Too much or too little publicity

YOUR LEADERSHIP STYLE CONSISTS OF:

THE ASSUMPTIONS YOU MAKE ABOUT YOUR EMPLOYEES

THE POWER YOU EITHER SHARE OR KEEP FOR YOURSELF

THE COMMUNICATION BEHAVIORS AND STYLES YOU PERFORM

128

THEORY X LEADERS ASSUME:

- PEOPLE ARE NATURALLY LAZY

- PEOPLE LACK AMBITION AND DISLIKE RESPONSIBILITY

- PEOPLE ARE SELF-CENTERED, NOT ORGANIZATION-CENTERED

- PEOPLE NATURALLY RESIST CHANGE

THEREFORE:

PEOPLE MUST BE PERSUADED, REWARDED, PUNISHED,

CONTROLLED, AND DIRECTED.

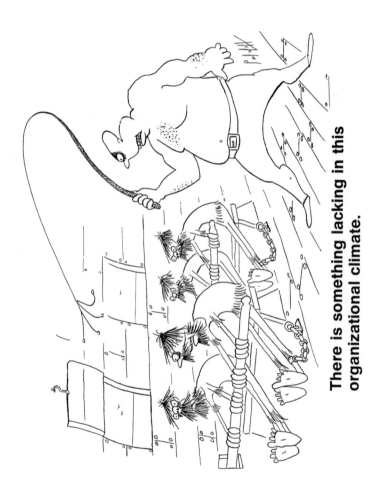

There is something lacking in this organizational climate.

THEORY Y LEADERS ASSUME:

- PEOPLE ARE NATURALLY ACTIVE

- PEOPLE DERIVE SATISFACTION FROM WORK ITSELF

- PEOPLE ARE INTERESTED IN ORGANIZATION AND SELF

- PEOPLE PROMOTE CHANGE THEY UNDERSTAND AND SUPPORT

- PEOPLE TIRE OF MONOTONY

- PEOPLE CONSTANTLY GROW

THEREFORE:

PEOPLE MUST BE GIVEN RESPONSIBILITY, VARIETY, SUPPORT, INFORMATION, AND OPPORTUNITIES FOR GROWTH.

THEORY X LEADERS AND THEORY Y LEADERS

ARE BOTH RIGHT.   WHY?

A LEADER'S ASSUMPTIONS AND EXPECTATIONS
ARE TRANSMITTED BY:

"CLIMATE"
FEEDBACK
INPUT
OUTPUT
NONVERBAL CUES

USE OF POWER:

AUTOCRATIC LEADERS: KEEP IT

CONSULTATIVE LEADERS: KEEP IT, BUT ASK FOR INPUT

DEMOCRATIC LEADERS: SHARE IT

LAISSEZ-FAIRE LEADERS: GIVE IT AWAY

AMOUNT OF
POWER

ALL

NONE

TYPE OF
LEADERSHIP

AUTOCRATIC CONSULTATIVE DEMOCRATIC LAISSEZ-FAIRE

THE AUTOCRAT:

- COMMUNICATES DOWNWARD

- ORDERS, INFORMS AND INSTRUCTS

- PROMOTES MAXIMUM EFFICIENCY

- IS MOST EFFECTIVE WHEN:

  THERE IS NO EMERGENCY

  FOLLOWERS LACK KNOWLEDGE

  FOLLOWERS DON'T CARE

  FOLLOWERS EXPECT AUTOCRATIC LEADERSHIP

THE CONSULTANT:

- COMMUNICATES DOWNWARD AND UPWARD

- ASKS, THEN DECIDES

- PROMOTES FOLLOWER COMMITMENT

- IS MOST EFFECTIVE WHEN:

  SOME TIME IS AVAILABLE

  FOLLOWERS HAVE KNOWLEDGE TO CONTRIBUTE

  FOLLOWERS WANT TO CONTRIBUTE

  WHEN FOLLOWER COMMITMENT IS IMPORTANT

THE DEMOCRAT:

- COMMUNICATES PRIMARILY UPWARD

- SHARES POWER EQUALLY (1 PERSON-1 VOTE)

- ENHANCES MORALE BUT REDUCES EFFICIENCY

- IS MOST EFFECTIVE WHEN:

  MUCH TIME IS AVAILABLE

  FOLLOWERS ARE KNOWLEDGEABLE AND MOTIVATED

  GROUP GOALS ARE CLEAR AND ACCEPTED

  GROUP MEMBERS LIKE ONE ANOTHER

THE LAISSEZ-FAIRE:

- DOES NOT COMMUNICATE

- EXERTS NO POWER

- MAXIMIZES PARTICIPATION

- IS MOST EFFECTIVE WHEN:

  MAXIMUM TIME IS AVAILABLE

  FOLLOWERS ARE KNOWLEDGEABLE AND MOTIVATED

  GROUP GOALS ARE CLEAR AND ACCEPTED

  THE GROUP IS WORKING WELL

TYPES OF COMMUNICATION STYLES

OSTRICH: "HEAD IN THE SAND"

COUNTRY CLUB: "IS EVERYBODY HAPPY"?

HARD NOSE: "SHAPE UP OR SHIP OUT"

MIDDLE OF THE ROAD: "LET'S DO WHAT WE CAN"

TEAM LEADER: "ONE FOR ALL; ALL FOR ONE"

Probable Effect of Pure Style on:	Ostrich	Country Club	Hard Nose	Middle of the Road	Team Management
Typical Phrase	• "Don't rock the boat."	• "People first."	• "Get the job done or get out."	• "Do what we can."	• "Together we can win."
Assumption Concerning Production – People Interaction	• Most people just want to draw a paycheck. • Minimum performance is all that is necessary and expected.	• Work is by-product of satisfied people. • Take care of the people and work takes care of itself.	• Nothing counts except production. • People must be bribed or forced. • People are paid to take orders and to work.	• People will give a fair day's work for a fair day's pay.	• People will work hard to accomplish goals they have helped establish.
Commitment	• Low • Little commitment on part of manager or his group.	• Low to high • Committed within people reference only; not for productivity.	• Low in long run • Little individual commitment except through fear.	• Medium to high • Solid but not outstanding.	• High • Individual goals aligned with organization goals.
Conflict	• Avoid	• Smooth over • Conflict hurts people.	• Suppress • Conflict assumed	• Compromise • Political solution is possible.	• Examine and use • Normal for organizations, but may be handled creatively.
Communication	• Low • Only routine announcements and other required information.	• Up and down • People relations	• Downward and across • Job related • Usually "Tell"	• Up, down, and across • Encouraged • Balance between people and production matters.	• Up, down, and across • Encouraged and creative. • People and Production matters.
Creativity	• Low expectations.	• Low for productivity matters. • High for people matters.	• Very little spontaneous creativity generated. "Beat the system." Creativity often high & ingenious.	• Medium • Generated & encouraged for both people and production matters.	• High • All levels encouraged and recognized.
Relationships	• Isolated — No real relationships develop.	• Good • Based on people matters.	• Rough. Can get backbiting through fear. • Based on production matters.	• Good • Balance between people and production matters.	• Dynamic • Based on mutual goals and trust.
Development of Subordinates	• Usually little. • Good people leave. • Sometimes a rebel is developed.	• Poor • Not results-oriented.	• Poor • Little chance for personnel initiative except for chosen few.	• Good • Limited opportunity for person to innovate.	• Excellent. • The ideal learning situation.

Listed below are several things which you may do when you communicate with the people who report to you. *Circle the number* which best indicates the extent to which you do each of the behaviors described when you communicate with your subordinates.

Key:

5   To a very great extent
4   To a great extent
3   To some extent
2   To a little extent
1   To a very little extent

Tells employees what to do and how to do it.	5	4	3	2	1
Gives employees the information they want.	5	4	3	2	1
Asks employees to participate in making decisions.	5	4	3	2	1
Promotes happy relations among employees.	5	4	3	2	1
Stresses organizational goals and employees' roles in achieving them.	5	4	3	2	1
Is receptive to employees' ideas and suggestions.	5	4	3	2	1
Is friendly toward employees.	5	4	3	2	1
Listens attentively to employees.	5	4	3	2	1
Shows genuine concern for employees' well-being.	5	4	3	2	1
Tells employees how well they are doing their jobs.	5	4	3	2	1
Tells employees what is expected of them in their work.	5	4	3	2	1
Compliments employees who do good work.	5	4	3	2	1
Expresses sincere appreciation for employees' efforts.	5	4	3	2	1
Takes criticism from employees without resentment.	5	4	3	2	1
Gets back to employees when promises to.	5	4	3	2	1
Treats employees with respect.	5	4	3	2	1
Keeps the promises he/she makes to employees.	5	4	3	2	1
Explains the reasons for changes which are made.	5	4	3	2	1
Tells employees about happenings in other areas or departments of the organization.	5	4	3	2	1
Really seems to understand how employees feel.	5	4	3	2	1

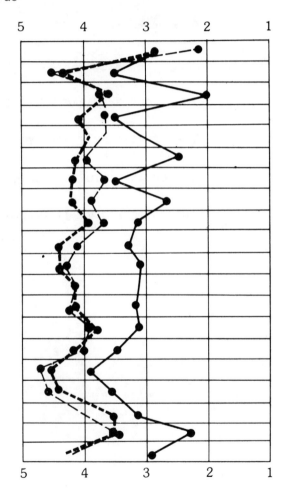

Key:

What employees say their supervisors do	————————
What employees prefer their supervisors do	‑ ‑ ‑ ‑ ‑ ‑ ‑
What supervisors think they do	— — — — —

WHERE DOES YOUR OWN LEADERSHIP STYLE COME FROM?

1. YOUR PERSONALITY

2. YOUR LIFE PHILOSOPHY

3. YOUR GROUP'S CHARACTERISTICS

4. YOUR RELATIONSHIP WITH YOUR GROUP

5. YOUR ORGANIZATION'S REQUIREMENTS

6. YOUR SOCIETY'S VALUE SYSTEM

TO IMPROVE YOUR COMMUNICATION STYLE:

1. GET FEEDBACK FROM MEMBERS

2. ASK MEMBERS' PREFERENCES

3. ADJUST TO PREFERENCES AS APPROPRIATE

PARTICIPATIVE PROBLEM-SOLVING

MEANS: -Collective responsibility for problems
         -Involvement in problem identification and analysis
         -Involvement in solution development and implementation

DOES NOT MEAN: -Employees "run the place"
                 -Decision-making is given up by management
                 -The organization becomes a democracy

BRINGS ABOUT: -Better communication
                -Collective ownership
                -Improved trust
                -Team work
                -Creativity
                -Productivity
                -Morale

146

To make PARTICIPATIVE LEADERSHIP work, you must:

1. Prove you believe in it

2. Have employees who believe in it

3. Use their recommendations

4. Ask about important matters

5. Ask about relevant matters (for everyone)

6. Ask about matters known to the group

7. Ask a little at a time

8. Minimize the status distinction

9. RELAX

To Generate Participation and Discussion:

1. Use non-directed questions

2. Use directed questions
    - Be certain person can answer
    - Require more than yes/no
    - Pass it around
    - Monitor nonverbal feedback

3. Use redirected questions

4. Cut off the verbose; encourage the shy

5. Divide, assign, and report

TO COPE WITH CONFLICT:

    LOOK FOR IT

    ANALYZE IT: SUBSTANDE OR PERSONALITY?

    DEAL WITH IT

    TALK ABOUT FEELINGS

    ENCOURAGE COMPROMISE

    EMPHASIZE GROUP GOALS

    AVOID TAKING SIDES

To CRITICIZE CONSTRUCTIVELY:

BE CLEAR

BE RELEVANT

BE TIMELY

BE HELPFUL

BE REASONABLE

BE KIND . . . .

COALITIONS

OCCUR WHEN A SUBGROUP FORMS

HINDER WHEN THEY DISTRACT OR DISRUPT

CONTROLLABLE THROUGH

- DIRECT QUESTIONS

- GOAL EMPHASIS

- TASK ASSIGNMENT

- ROLE PLAYING

GROUPTHINK

SIGNS: NO DISAGREEMENT

HIGH COHESIVENESS

HIGH CONFORMITY

PERCEIVED INFALLIBILITY

SOLUTIONS: ENCOURAGE ALTERNATIVES

PLAY DEVIL'S ADVOCATE

LOOK FOR OUTSIDE OPINIONS

ENCOURAGE RE-EXAMINATION

HIDDEN AGENDA: GOALS BESIDES THE GROUP GOAL WHICH ARE

                  HELD BY INDIVIDUAL MEMBERS

    FOR EXAMPLE: AVOID WORK

                  SOCIALIZE

                  IMPROVE PROMOTABILITY

AS LEADER: WATCH FOR CONFLICTING GROUP/INDIVIDUAL GOALS

                  INTEGRATE INDIVIDUAL GOALS

                  DEAL WITH INDIVIDUALS PRIVATELY AS NEEDED

                  MAKE INDIVIDUAL GOALS AN AGENDA ITEM
                  FOR DISCUSSION

HOW MUCH CONTROL SHOULD YOU EXERT OVER THE MEETING?

A. WHAT DOES THE GROUP EXPECT YOU TO DO?
   - INITIALLY, MEET THEIR EXPECTATIONS

B. WHAT IS THE PURPOSE OF THE MEETING?
   - MAKE YOUR CONTROL FIT THE SITUATION

C. WHAT METHODS IS THE GROUP USING?
   - SOME PROCEDURES NEED CONTROL, OTHERS DON'T

D. HOW EXPERIENCED ARE THE MEMBERS?
   - INEXPERIENCED MEMBERS NEED CONTROL MORE.

E. WHAT ARE YOUR SKILL AND CONFIDENCE LEVELS?
   - A SHORTAGE OF EITHER MAKES CONTROL NECESSARY

F. HOW MUCH TIME IS AVAILABLE?
   - WITHOUT CONTROL, HASTE IS A WASTE

G. HOW INVOLVED ARE THE GROUP MEMBERS?
   - MORE INVOLVEMENT REQUIRES LESS CONTROL

AS A GENERAL RULE: START WITH TIGHT CONTROL, AND
                     GRADUALLY GIVE IT AWAY

Leader Checklist for Successful Meetings

_____ Meeting place has been arranged.

_____ Meeting time has been arranged.

_____ Audio-visual equipment.

     _____ Accessible outlets

     _____ Extension cords

     _____ Designated operator

_____ Handouts

_____ Visual aids

     _____ Flip pads

     _____ Charts

     _____ Graphs

     _____ Photos

     _____ Chalkboard

_____ Writing materials

     _____ Note pads

     _____ Pens or pencils

_____ Expected guests or guestspeakers

_____ Seating arrangement

     _____ Is the recorder close to you since you may need to interact with him or her frequently?

     _____ Are group members who serve on the same committee seated adjacently so as to facilitate their interaction?

     _____ Is there extra seating for guests?

DURING THE MEETING:

1. INITIATE THE DISCUSSION

2. KEEP THE DISCUSSION ORDERLY

3. EQUALIZE PARTICIPATION

4. STIMULATE CREATIVE & CRITICAL THINKING

5. FACILITATE MUTUAL UNDERSTANDING

6. PROMOTE COOPERATIVE RELATIONSHIPS

7. DEVELOP GROUP AND MEMBERS

TO INITIATE:

ANNOUNCE TOPIC OR PURPOSE

REVIEW PREVIOUS MEETINGS

DISTRIBUTE ANY OUTLINES, MATERIALS

ESTABLISH INFORMAL ATMOSPHERE

ANNOUNCE RULES OF PROCEDURE

SELECT A RECORDER

TO MAINTAIN ORDER:

MAKE PROCEDURES PUBLIC/VISIBLE

KEEP GROUP ORIENTED

WATCH FOR DEVIATIONS

RECORD IDEAS

SUMMARIZE PROGRESS

PROVIDE TRANSITIONS

WHEN REPITITION OCCURS, MOVE ON

BE SURE IMPORTANT MATTERS ARE THOROUGHLY DISCUSSED

WATCH TIME

CONCLUDE CLEARLY

TO EQUALIZE PARTICIPATION:

STRESS IMPORTANCE OF EQUITY

SPEAK TO GROUP, NOT INDIVIDUALS

CONTROL TALKATIVE MEMBERS

ENCOURAGE QUIET MEMBERS

LISTEN TO CONTRIBUTIONS

BE ALERT TO MEMBERS WANTING TO TALK

RE-DIRECT QUESTIONS

REACT NONVERBALLY

<u>TO STIMULATE</u>:

POSTPONE DECISION-MAKING

TEST EVIDENCE

EXAMINE ASSUMPTIONS

TEST PROPOSALS

AVOID "YES-NO" QUESTIONS

DEAL WITH SPECIFIC PIECES, NOT WHOLES

WATCH FOR NEW AREAS OF THOUGHT

TO FACILITATE UNDERSTANDING:

CHECK FOR UNDERSTANDING

PARAPHRASE

ASK OTHER MEMBERS FOR EXAMPLES, ELABORATION

BE SENSITIVE TO NEW VIEWPOINTS

TO PROMOTE COOPERATION:

WATCH FOR HIDDEN AGENDA

EMPHASIZE IMPORTANCE OF MUTUAL ACCEPTANCE

KEEP CONFLICTS SUSTANTIVE, NOT PERSONAL

PROMOTE ENJOYMENT

BREAK DEADLOCKS THROUGH
- SYNTHESIZED SOLUTIONS
- COMPROMISE
- NEED FULFILLMENT

TO PROMOTE GROUP & INDIVIDUAL DEVELOPMENT:

DISCUSS GROUP PERFORMANCE AT END OF MEETING

ASK FOR FEEDBACK RE. LEADERSHIP

GIVE FEEDBACK RE. PARTICIPATION

REQUEST REVIEW BY FACILITATOR

USE BOTH PUBLIC PROCESSING AND PRIVATE QUESTIONNAIRES

Meeting Effectiveness Questionnaire

Circle the number that best describes how you would rate the effectiveness of the meeting.

Key: 1 — Sharply Disagree;   2 — Disagree;   3 — Neutral
4 — Agree;   5 — Sharply Agree

1. I clearly understood the purpose of the meeting.   1 2 3 4 5
2. The persons who were most directly involved with the purpose of the meeting were in attendance.   1 2 3 4 5
3. All persons present had the opportunity to participate by expressing their views and opinions.   1 2 3 4 5
4. I had sufficient time to prepare for the meeting.   1 2 3 4 5
5. The leader of the meeting maintained the focus in the purpose, not in side issues.   1 2 3 4 5
6. I can easily support the results of the meeting because I understand clearly what is expected of me.   1 2 3 4 5
7. The leader of the meeting was open to all ideas that were presented.   1 2 3 4 5
8. I understood what was expected of me during the meeting.   1 2 3 4 5
9. Ideas that were presented were clarified and readily understood by all present.   1 2 3 4 5
10. I understood the ideas that were presented during the meeting.   1 2 3 4 5
11. The participants who were present wanted to work for the best interests of the group.   1 2 3 4 5
12. At the conclusion of the meeting, it was obvious to me that everyone knew what was expected of them.   1 2 3 4 5
13. The proper amount of time was allocated for the meeting.   1 2 3 4 5
14. The agenda/topics of the meeting were displayed so all persons present could see them.   1 2 3 4 5
15. The agenda/topics were prioritized with the most important topics coming first.   1 2 3 4 5
16. Important ideas were recorded, thereby retaining valuable information for future use.   1 2 3 4 5
17. At the conclusion of the meeting, time was allocated to review the effectiveness of the meeting.   1 2 3 4 5

DISCUSSION PARTICIPATION EVALUATION

For _____

Instructions: Circle the number which best reflects your evaluation of the discussant's participation on each scale.

Superior   Poor

1 2 3 4 5   1. Was prepared and informed.

1 2 3 4 5   2. Contributions were brief and clear.

1 2 3 4 5   3. Comments relevant and well timed.

1 2 3 4 5   4. Spoke distinctly and audibly to all.

1 2 3 4 5   5. Contributions made readily and voluntarily.

1 2 3 4 5   6. Frequency of participation (if poor, too low ( ) or high ( ).

1 2 3 4 5   7. Nonverbal responses were clear and constant.

1 2 3 4 5   8. Listened to understand and follow discussion.

1 2 3 4 5   9. Openminded.

1 2 3 4 5 10. Cooperative and constructive.

1 2 3 4 5 11. Helped keep discussion organized, following outline.

1 2 3 4 5 12. Contributed to evaluation of information and ideas.

1 2 3 4 5 13. Respectful and tactful with others.

1 2 3 4 5 14. Encouraged others to participate.

1 2 3 4 5 15. Assisted in leadership functions.

1 2 3 4 5 16. Overall rating in relation to other discussants.

Comments:

Evaluator _____

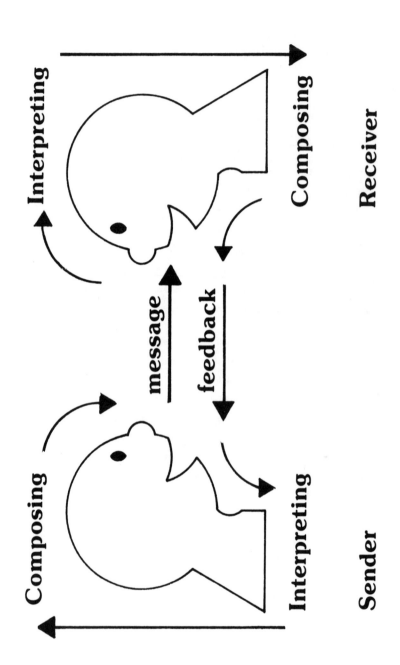

Interpreting

Composing

Receiver

message

feedback

Composing

Interpreting

Sender

POOR LISTENING HABITS:

1. PRIVATE PLANNING

2. AVOIDING COMPLICATED INFORMATION

3. SELF-DEBATING

4. PREMATURE BOREDOM

5. OTHER-CONSCIOUSNESS

6. MISSING "BIG PICTURE"

7. PERSONAL BIAS

8. MENTAL HOLIDAY

RESULTS: POINTS MISSED

MISTAKES MADE

TIME WASTED

LISTENER REJECTED

167

TO GENUINELY HEAR THE PERSON SPEAKING TO YOU, YOU MUST:

BE <u>H</u>ELPFUL

BE <u>EM</u>PATHETIC

BE <u>A</u>TTENTIVE

BE <u>R</u>ESPONSIVE

To improve the HELPFULNESS dimension:

1. Minimize waiting time

2. Maximize meeting time

3. Deformalize the environment

4. Make the environment attractive

5. Prevent potential distractions

6. Encourage future meetings

To improve the EMPATHY dimension:

1. Ask about the person
2. Paraphrase
3. Reflect perceived feelings
4. Deformalize the environment
5. Use touch (carefully)

To improve the ATTENTIVENESS dimension:

1. Suspend reactions

2. Withhold judgment and emotions

3. Avoid interruptions

4. Show understanding before disagreeing

5. Summarize periodically

6. Use echoing

To improve the RESPONSIVENESS dimension:

1. Maintain eye contact
2. Use nonverbal reinforcement
3. Use vocal prompts
4. Use attentive posture
5. Ask questions
6. Stop talking

To LISTEN EFFECTIVELY,

ACTIVELY ASK FOR INFORMATION OF INTEREST . . .

PARAPHRASE WHAT YOU THINK YOU HEARD . . .

ENCOURAGE THE SPEAKER TO TALK . . .

REFLECT HOW YOU THINK THE SPEAKER FEELS . . .

THINK BEFORE CONCLUDING AND REACTING . . .

SUMMARIZE MENTALLY MAJOR POINTS COVERED . . .

AND ABOVE ALL:

WORK AT BEING A GOOD LISTENER.

To Send Messages Effectively,

BEWARE OF BYPASSING

- MAKE SURE THAT YOUR WORDS MEAN THE SAME THINGS TO
  EVERYONE ELSE THAT THEY DO TO YOU.

STAMP OUT STEREOTYPES

- AVOID ASSUMING MANY CHARACTERISTICS ON THE BASIS OF
  JUST ONE THAT YOU HAVE OBSERVED.

PULVERIZE POLARIZING

- RECOGNIZE GRAY AREAS BETWEEN THE BLACK AND WHITE;
  ALLOW COMPROMISE BETWEEN EXTREMES.

EVADE EMOTIONALIZING

- CHOOSE WORDS WHICH ARE NOT EMOTIONALLY LOADED,
  NOT WORDS WHICH WILL CAUSE A KNEE-JERK RESPONSE.

NONVERBAL COMMUNICATION INCLUDES:

- THE ENVIRONMENT

- PROXEMICS

- POSTURES

- GESTURES

- HEAD/FACE/EYES

- VOICE

175

POSTURE WORKS FOR YOU WHEN:

    YOU SIT IN AN "OPEN" POSTURE

    YOU SIT UP, NOT SLOUCHED

    YOU FACE THE OTHER PERSON

HEAD/FACE/EYES WORK FOR YOU WHEN:

    YOU ARE ACTIVE AND RESPONSIVE

    YOU MAINTAIN EYE CONTACT

    YOU ARE EXPRESSIVE

TO USE NONVERBAL CUES PROPERLY, BE:

DIRECT

ACTIVE

CONSISTENT

SPONTANEOUS

<u>COMPARED TO INDIVIDUALS, GROUPS:</u>

- HAVE MORE IDEAS & KNOWLEDGE

- ARE MORE CREATIVE

- ARE MORE OBJECTIVE

- GET MORE DONE IF LABOR DIVIDED

BUT THEY ALSO:

- ARE MORE EASILY DISTRACTED

- ARE SLOWER IN DECISION-MAKING

- CAN INHIBIT MEMBERS

GROUPS WORK BEST WHEN:

1) THERE IS NO ONE RIGHT SOLUTION

2) LABOR CAN BE DIVIDED

3) GOALS ARE SOMEWHAT UNCLEAR

4) MANY POSSIBLE SOLUTIONS ARE AVAILABLE

5) MEMBER COMMITMENT IS IMPORTANT

6) QUALITY IS MORE IMPORTANT THAN SPEED

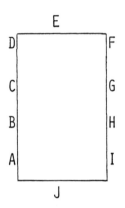

1. WHO IS LIKELY TO BE LEADER?

2. WHO IS MOST LIKELY TO BE LEFT OUT?

3. WHICH PAIRS ARE MOST LIKELY TO TALK TO EACH OTHER?

4. WHICH ARRANGEMENT BELOW IS BEST?   WHY?

A.   B.   C.   D.

GROUP NORMS ARE UNDERSTOOD RULES ABOUT MEMBERS' BEHAVIOR,
SUCH AS:

- DO WE SHOW UP ON TIME?

- ARE WE ABSENT OFTEN?

- HOW FAST DO WE WORK?

- DO WE INTERRUPT OR TAKE TURNS?

- WHERE/WHEN DO WE MEET?

- HOW DO WE TREAT EACH OTHER?

WHEN RULES ARE BROKEN, MEMBERS:

- DELAY

- COMMUNICATE MORE

- KID

- PERSUADE

- ABUSE

- THREATEN

- REJECT

Group norms tend to set the pace.

TO IMPROVE GROUP SPIRIT:

INCREASE DIRECTNESS

FIND SIMILARITIES

FIND COMPLIMENTARY NEEDS

PROVIDE REINFORCEMENT

SHARE COMMON EXPERIENCES

GROUP ROLES:

TASK   INITIATOR

                               INFORMATION SEEKER

                               ENERGIZER

                               ORIENTER

                               SECRETARY

SOCIAL   ENCOURAGER

                               HARMONIZER

                               COMEDIAN

                               GATEKEEPER

                               FOLLOWER

SELF-CENTERED   BLOCKER

                               AGGRESSOR

                               PLAYBOY

                               SELF CONFESSOR

                               HELPSEEKER

                               SPECIAL INTEREST PLEADER

184

<u>GROUP CONSENSUS IS HELPED BY</u>:

ACTIVE PARTICIPATION

GROUP SPIRIT

CONFLICT RESOLUTION

COMMUNICATION WHICH IS: GOAL ORIENTED

                                 OBJECTIVE

                                 INFORMED

                                 RELEVANT

                                 AGREEING

TO CONTRIBUTE TO YOUR GROUP:

BE INFORMED

BE COOPERATIVE

BE OPEN-MINDED

BE RATIONAL

BE ACTIVE

BE OBSERVANT

BE PATIENT

186

Self-Actualization

Esteem of Self and Colleagues

Social Interaction

Safe Environment

Physiological Well-being

<u>TO OVERCOME APATHY</u>:

FORM VOLUNTARY GROUPS

PLAY DEVIL'S ADVOCATE

GIVE RESPONSIBILITY

ADDRESS MEMBER DIRECTLY

USE "METADISCUSSION"

BE SUPPORTIVE

SIGNS OF HOSTILITY INCLUDE:

MONOPOLIZING DISCUSSION

INVOKING AUTHORITY

NEGATIVISM

DOGMATIC BEHAVIOR

OFFENSIVE BEHAVIOR

AND

DESTRUCTIVE HUMOR

MORALIZATION

CRITICISM

GOSSIPING

IRRELEVANT COMMENTS

DEFENSIVENESS

OCCURS WHEN A THREAT IS PERCEIVED DUE TO:

- EVALUATIVE BEHAVIOR

- CONTROL-ORIENTED BEHAVIOR

- STRATEGIC BEHAVIOR

- NEUTRAL BEHAVIOR

- SUPERIORISTIC BEHAVIOR

- DOGMATIC BEHAVIOR

TO AVOID IT, BE:

DESCRIPTIVE

PROBLEM-ORIENTED

SPONTANEOUS

EMPATHIC

EQUALISTIC

PROVISIONAL

SIGNS OF AGGRESSION INCLUDE:

ARGUING

COMPLAINING

GOSSIPING

MARTYRDOM

INTERRUPTING

NAME CALLING

CHALLENGING INTEGRITY

"BRUSH OFF"

PROBLEM-SOLVING PHASES:

1. identify and define current problem issues.

2. determine which issues are of primary importance.

3. list all possible causes underlying that issue.

4. identify the most important causes.

5. generate a list of possible solutions.

6. determine which possible solutions seem preferable.

7. arrive at the best possible solution.

8. develop an action plan whereby that solution can be implemented.

| | Issues | Priority Rankings | |
		Own	Group
1.			
2.			
3.			
4.			
5.			
6.			
7.			
8.			
9.			
10.			
11.			
12.			

TO IDENTIFY A REAL PROBLEM, ASK:

1. IS PROBLEM REALLY JUST A <u>SYMPTOM</u> OF A LARGER ONE?

2. WHAT ARE THE <u>EFFECTS</u> OF THE PROBLEM?

3. WHO CAN <u>FIX</u> IT?

4. WHAT IS <u>HAPPENING</u> <u>NOW</u> TO FIX IT?

5. WHAT HAPPENS IF IT IS <u>NOT</u> <u>FIXED</u>?

TYPES OF PROBLEMS

TYPE <u>A</u>:   WE CAN FIX IT

TYPE <u>B</u>:   WE CAN, WITH OTHERS' HELP

TYPE <u>C</u>:   SOMEONE ELSE CAN FIX IT

TYPE <u>D</u>:   NO ONE CAN FIX IT

INFORMATION CAN BE GATHERED BY:

- SURVEYS AND QUESTIONNAIRES

- INTERVIEWS OR MEETINGS WITH EXPERTS

- RESEARCH OF PUBLIC SOURCES

- RESEARCH OF ORGANIZATIONAL SOURCES, SUCH AS:

  ACCOUNTING

  PERSONNEL

  QUALITY ASSURANCE/QUALITY CONTROL

  PURCHASING

  SALES AND MARKETING

  MAINTENANCE

  ENGINEERING

- PERSONAL OBSERVATION AND MEASUREMENT

FLOW PROCESS CHART

SUMMARY CHART

	Real	Ideal	Difference
O Operation	7		
T Transportation	8		
I Inspection	1		
D Delay	3		
S Storage	0		
Distance	740 ft		
Time	38'		

JOB CHARTED: Handling valuables of semi-private & private patients

PERFORMED BY: Nurse

CHARTED BY: _____

Process begins At nurses' station

Process ends At nurses' station

	EVENT	TYPE	DIST.	TIME	NOTES
1	Gets envelope & form	O⊠ T I D S		1'	At 3rd floor nurses' station
2	Fills in information	O⊠ T I D S		1'	
3	Walks to patient room	O ⊠ I D S	30 ft	½'	
4	Checks valuables w/ pat.	O T ⊠ D S		5'	
5	Records amt. & kind of valuables on form & envlp	O⊠ T I D S		2'	
6	Signs temp. receipt	O⊠ T I D S		½'	
7	Gives temp. receipt to patient	O⊠ T I D S		½'	
8	Walks to elevator	O ⊠ I D S	180 ft	3'	
9	Waits for elevator	O T I ⊠ S		3'	
10	Rides to main floor	O⊠ T I D S	35 ft	2'	
11	Walks to cashier	O ⊠ I D S	125 ft	2'	
12	Gives valuables to cash.	O⊠ T I D S		½'	
13	Waits while val's checked & perm. receipt given	O T I ⊠ S		7'	
14	Walks to elevator	O ⊠ I D S	125 ft	2'	
15	Waits for elevator	O T I ⊠ S		3'	
16	Rides to 3rd floor	O⊠ I D S	35 ft	2'	
17	Walks to pat. room	O⊠ I D S	180 ft	3'	

197

TO DEVELOP A DATA DISPLAY:

1. DECIDE WHAT IS TO BE MEASURED, AND WHY

2. DECIDE IN WHAT TIME PERIODS THE MEASURES WILL BE TAKEN

3. DECIDE WHAT THINGS ARE TO BE COMPARED (IF ANY) BY THE MEASURES

4. DEVELOP A CHECK SHEET FORM ON WHICH MEASURES CAN BE RECORDED

5. RECORD MEASURES DURING SELECTED TIME PERIOD(S)

6. DECIDE WHAT TYPE OF DISPLAY WILL BEST SHOW THE COLLECTED INFORMATION

7. DEVELOP THE DISPLAY

	1 Broken Wire	2 Blown Fuse	3 Cracked Mold	4 Faulty Connection	Total
Unit I	45	33	54	43	175
Unit II	13	17	14	6	50
Unit III	11	3	7	4	25
Total	69	53	75	53	250

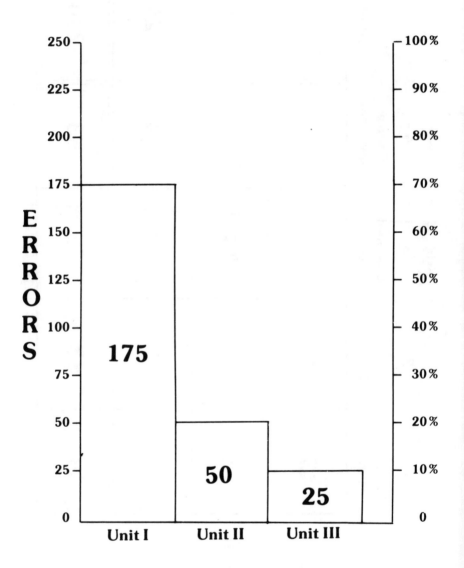

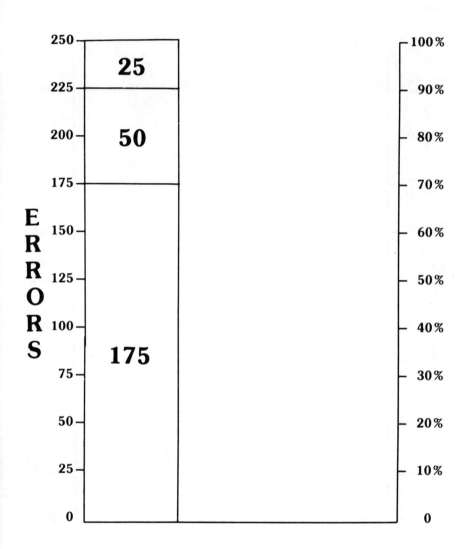

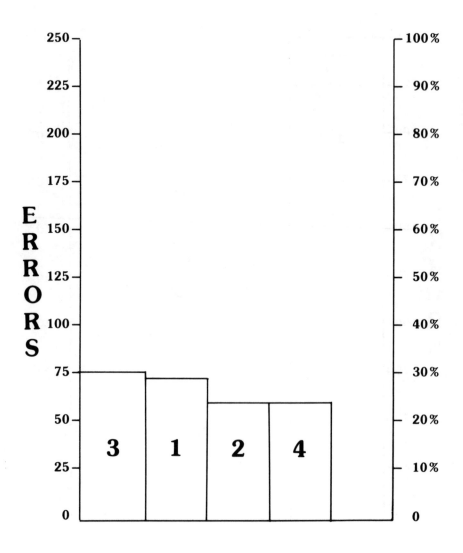

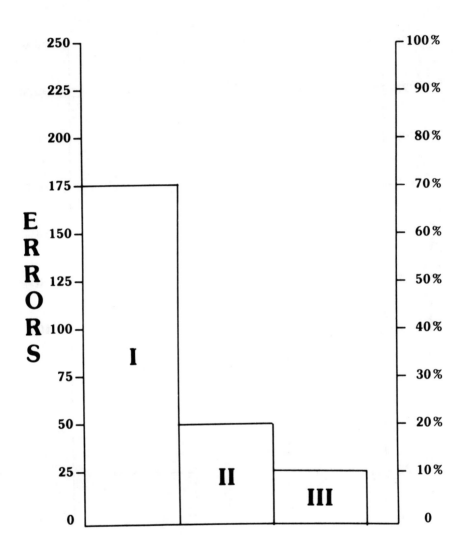

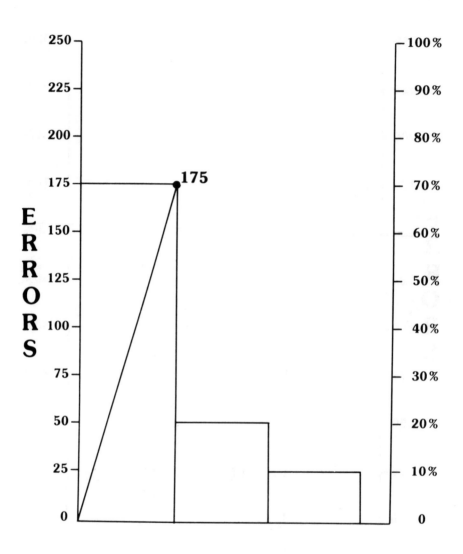

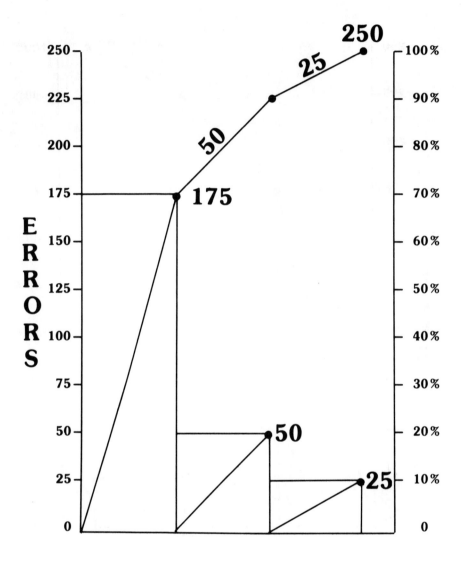

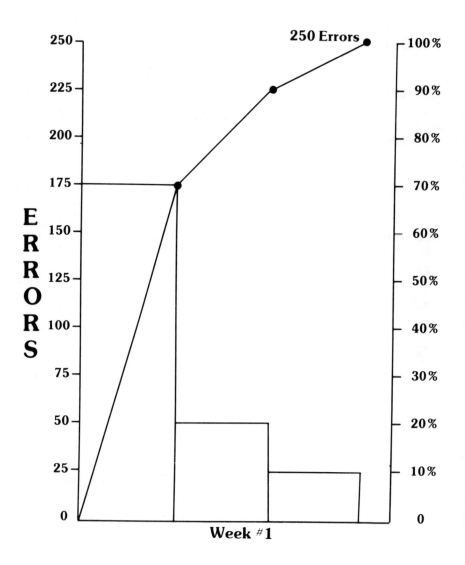

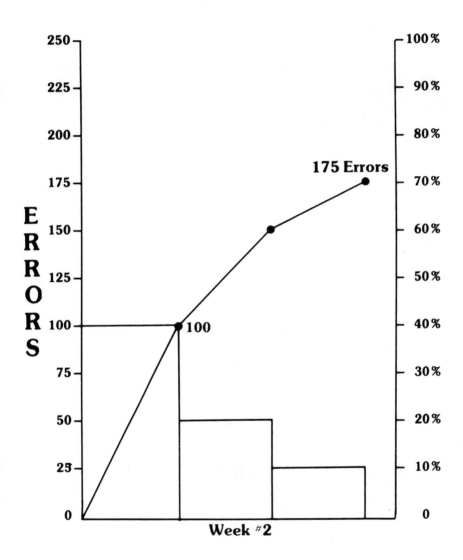

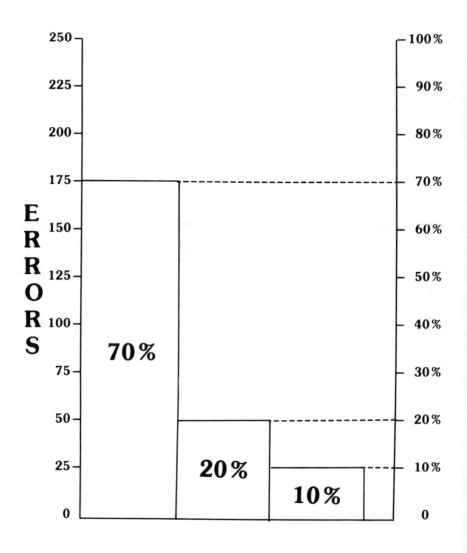

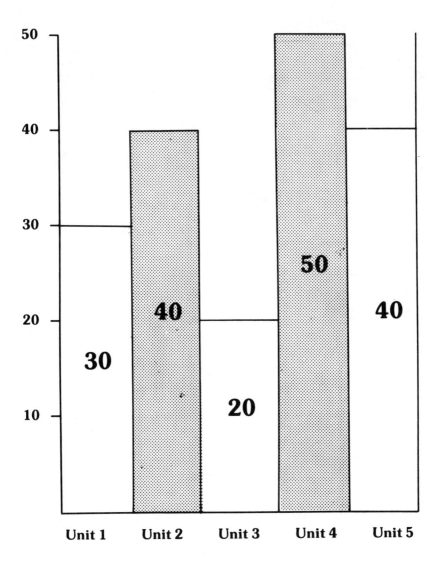

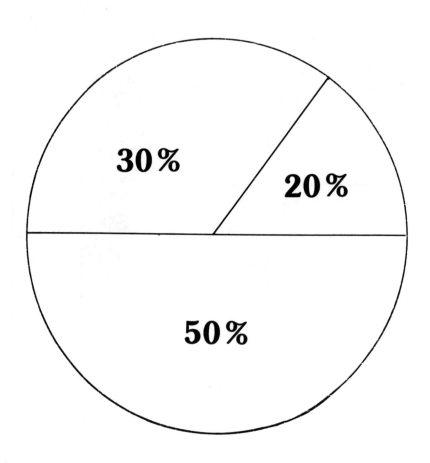

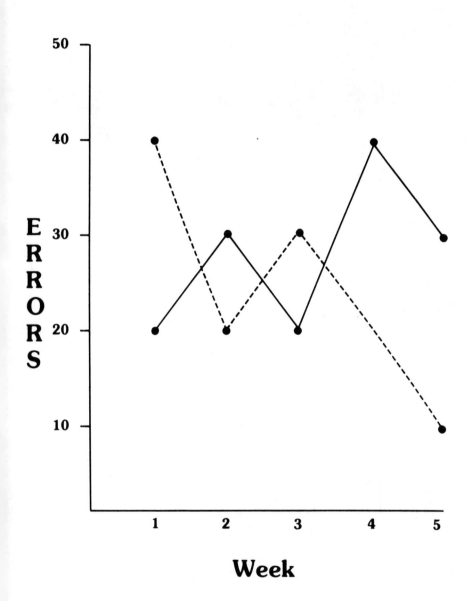

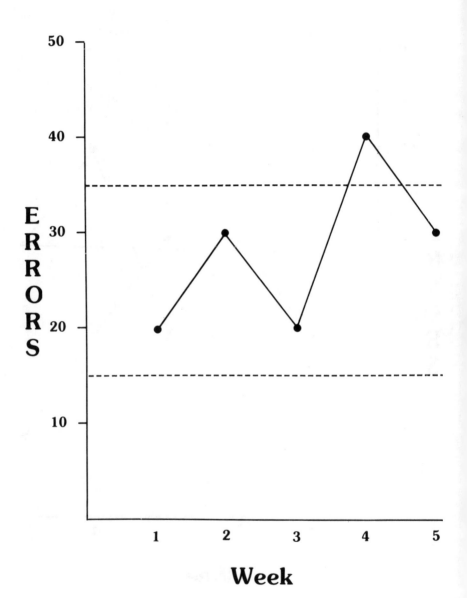

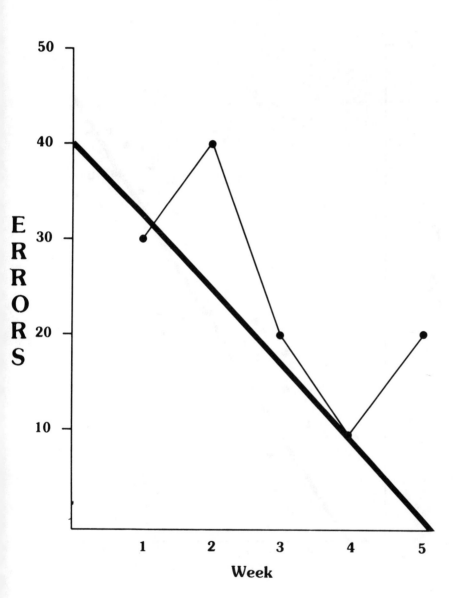

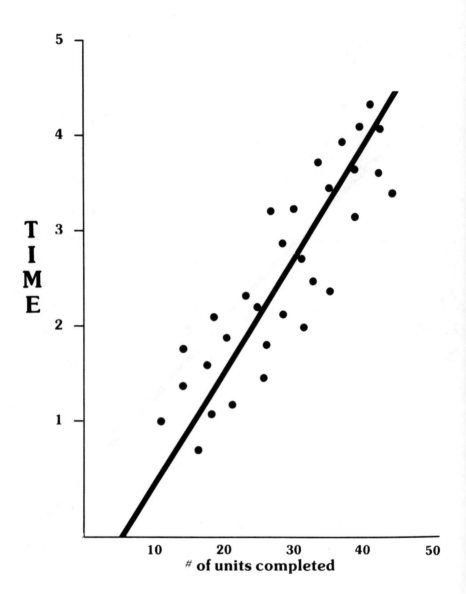

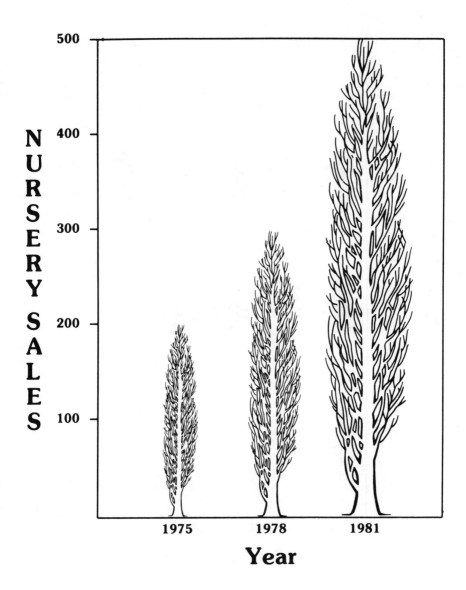

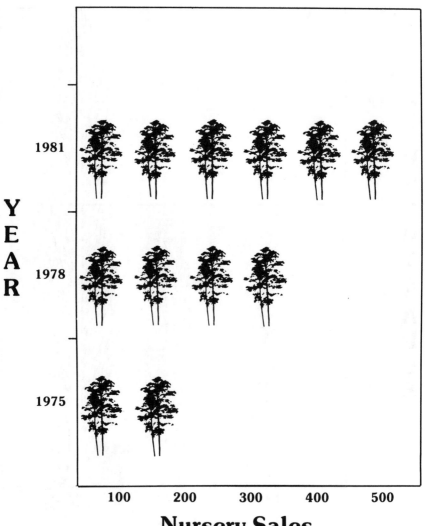

Y
E
A
R

1981

1978

1975

100   200   300   400   500

Nursery Sales

TO PRIORITIZE PROBLEMS:

1. HAVE GROUP VOTE ON THEM

2. HAVE GROUP RANK-ORDER THEM

3. HAVE GROUP RATE THEM

TO DETERMINE CAUSES:

1. LIST THE PROBLEM

2. BRAINSTORM FOR CAUSES

3. CATEGORIZE THE SUGGESTED CAUSES

4. SELECT THE MOST IMPORTANT CAUSES

5. RANK-ORDER THE SELECTED LIST

BRAINSTORMING

A. STATE THE PROBLEM

B. ELECT/APPOINT A RECORDER

C. REVIEW THE RULES
    1. FORGET FEASIBILITY
    2. BUILD ON OTHERS' IDEAS
    3. KEEP MOVING
    4. KILL CRITICISM

D. BRAINSTORM: INVITE/WRITE IDEAS

SILENT IDEA GENERATION

A. State the problem

B. Elect/appoint a recorder

C. Take 10 minutes to have all members write own ideas

D. Have each member in turn read one idea

E. As new ideas occur to members, they add to own list

F. Continue until all ideas exhausted

Possible Solutions

Preference Rankings

Own   Group

Possible Solutions	Own	Group
1.		
2.		
3.		
4.		
5.		
6.		
7.		
8.		
9.		
10.		
11.		
12.		
13.		
14.		
15.		
16.		
17.		
18.		
19.		
20.		

TO EVALUATE POSSIBLE SOLUTIONS, LOOK AT:

. COST
. TIME FOR IMPLEMENTATION
. SUPPORT NEEDED
. POTENTIAL RISKS
. ANTICIPATED SAVINGS
. PERSONNEL REQUIREMENTS
. POLITICAL RESISTANCE ANTICIPATED
. CONSISTENCY WITH ORGANIZATION'S OBJECTIVES
. POTENTIAL PRODUCTIVITY CHANGES

Evaluating Possible Solutions

Solution:
_____

Cost:

Time Required:

Support Needed:

Potential Risks:

Expected Savings/Advantages:

Personnel Requirements:

Anticipated Resistance:

Consistency with Objectives:

Solution:
_____

Cost:

Time Required:

Support Needed:

Potential Risks:

Expected Savings/Advantages:

Personnel Requirements:

Anticipated Resistance:

Consistency with Objectives:

Solution:
_____

Cost:

Time Required:

Support Needed:

Potential Risks:

Expected Savings/Advantages:

Personnel Requirements:

Anticipated Resistance:

Consistency with Objectives:

TO SELECT THE FINAL SOLUTION:

1. DISCUSS TO CONSENSUS

2. RATE ALTERNATIVES; CALCULATE AVERAGES

3. RANK ALTERNATIVES; CALCULATE AVERAGES

4. USE PROCESS OF ELIMINATION: "THE MURDER BOARD"

5. USE "LEAST LOST" PROCEDURE (ALL ADVANTAGES
     BEING EQUAL)

6. USE MAJORITY VOTE (AS A LAST, DESPERATE ACT)

ACTION PLAN

Activity	Staff Assigned	Support and/or Resources Needed	Coordination Needed	Evaluation Procedures	Start
1.					
2.					
3.					
4.					
5.					
6.					
7.					
8.					
9.					
10.					
11.					
12.					
13.					
14.					

QUALITY CIRCLE MEETING SEQUENCE

MEETING 1: IDENTIFYING PROBLEMS; BRAINSTORMING

MEETING 2: ANALYZING WORK; FLOW-PROCESS CHARTING

MEETING 3: GATHERING INFORMATION; ASSIGNING RESPONSIBILITIES

MEETING 4: DISPLAYING INFORMATION

MEETING 5: SELECTING PROBLEM; FISH-BONE DIAGRAMMING CAUSES

MEETING 6: SELECTING CAUSES

MEETING 7: BRAINSTORMING SOLUTIONS; SELECTING CANDIDATES

MEETING 8: EVALUATING POSSIBLE SOLUTIONS

MEETING 9: SELECTING SOLUTION

MEETING 10 AND CONTINUING: DEVELOPING ACTION PLANS

NOTE: SOME EVENTS MAY TAKE MORE THAN ONE MEETING;
       WHAT IS IMPORTANT IS THE SEQUENCE. AND PATIENCE.

226

THE MANAGEMENT PRESENTATION

I. PREPARATION   ANALYZE AUDIENCE
                                ORGANIZE MATERIALS
                                DEVELOP INTRODUCTION
                                DEVELOP CONCLUSION
                                DEVELOP AN OUTLINE
                                DEVELOP VISUAL AIDS

II. PRESENTATION   CONTROL NERVOUSNESS
                                USE NONVERBAL COMMUNICATION
                                USE VISUAL AIDS

III. HANDLING QUESTIONS

To Analyze Your Audience, Find Out:

1. What they are interested in

2. What they already know about your topic

3. How they feel about your topic -- their attitudes

4. What is important to them -- their values

This audience analysis tells you what things you can appeal to, what things you need to change, and what responses you can anticipate.

It should not tell you how to "tell them what they want to hear."

TYPES OF ORGANIZATIONAL PATTERNS

TYPE	DEFINITION
CHRONOLOGICAL	PRESENTED IN ORDER OF TIME
GEOGRAPHICAL	PRESENTED IN ORDER OF LOCATION
CAUSE-EFFECT	PRESENTED IN ORDER OF EVENTS OR FACTORS THAT BRING ABOUT OTHER EVENTS OR FACTORS
EFFECT-CAUSE	PRESENTED IN ORDER OF SYMPTOMS THAT SEEM TO HAVE BEEN BROUGHT ABOUT BY CERTAIN CAUSES
PROCESS	PRESENTED IN ORDER OF THE SEQUENCE BY WHICH SOMETHING IS DONE
QUESTION-ANSWER	PRESENTED IN ORDER OF QUESTIONS THE AUDIENCE IS LIKELY TO ASK, FOLLOWED BY ANSWERS
TOPICAL	PRESENTED IN ORDER OF NATURAL TOPICS AND SUBTOPICS
PROBLEM-SOLUTION	PRESENTED IN ORDER OF PROBLEMS IDENTIFIED, FOLLOWED BY SOLUTIONS PROPOSED

A GOOD INTRODUCTION: CAPTURES INTEREST
                        MOTIVATES LISTENING
                        BUILDS CREDIBILITY
                        PRESENTS PURPOSE

                THROUGH:

- A FAMOUS, THOUGHT-PROVOKING QUOTATION

- AN INTERESTING STORY OR ILLUSTRATION

- A DESCRIPTION OF IMPORTANT RECENT EVENTS

- A SERIES OF RHETORICAL QUESTIONS

- A STARTLING STATEMENT

- HUMOR

- STATEMENT OF THE TOPIC

CONCLUDING

Summary

Challenge or Appeal

Quotation

Illustration

Personal Endorsement

VISUAL AIDS

Object itself

Slides

Movies

Models

Maps

Graphs

Diagrams

Charts

GOOD VISUAL AIDS ARE:

Visible

Simple

Complete

Appropriate

Communicative

DO NOT STAND IN FRONT OF THE VISUAL AID.

TALK TO THE AUDIENCE, NOT THE AID.

KNOW THE AID WELL ENOUGH
THAT YOU DON'T HAVE TO STUDY IT
DURING THE PRESENTATION.

POINT TO THE PART OF THE AID
YOU ARE DISCUSSING.

TO CONTROL NERVOUSNESS:

1. USE MILD EXERCISE BEFORE THE SPEECH

2. SET REASONABLE GOALS FOR YOURSELF

3. MOVE WHILE SPEAKING

4. THINK ABOUT THE PRESENTATION

AVOID APPEARING EITHER . . .

TOO RELAXED, OR . . .

TOO TENSE.

239

YOU SPEAK MOST EFFECTIVELY WHEN YOU:

1. USE NATURAL BUT VARIED GESTURES WHILE SPEAKING

2. MOVE ABOUT WHILE TALKING

3. VARY YOUR VOCAL CHARACTERISTICS

4. ESTABLISH EYE CONTACT WITH EVERY LISTENER

WHEN USING PHYSICAL AIDS, HANDOUTS, OR DEMONSTRATIONS:

1. Practice
2. Be ready to "cover" for mishaps
3. Use audience participation
4. Pass around *during*; hand out after

WHEN USING CHARTS:

1. Position so that bottom edge is at least 4 feet above floor
2. Practice use of chart
3. Use "chart whispers"
4. Reveal/conceal
5. Do not stop at mid-chart

WHEN USING SLIDES:

1. Maintain a steady pace.
2. Use an average of 15 slides per 20 minutes.
3. Make duplicates if you must repeat same slide.
4. Show slide briefly before talking about it.
5. Read (where appropriate) all slide material.
6. Avoid turning your back; key slides to notes.
7. Do not put extremely complex material on slides.

WHEN USING OVERHEAD PROJECTORS:

1. Avoid "Keystoning".

2. Avoid light leaks.

3. Stand next to screen, not machine.

4. Do not let machine block view.

5. Do not stand in the way.

6. Point at screen, not machine.

7. Transfer quickly and smoothly.

WHEN USING CHALKBOARDS OR FLIP-PADS:

1. Plan words in advance
2. Write abbreviated, single ideas
3. Print
4. Enumerate
5. Stand sideways if writing while talking
6. Use a variety of symbols
7. Use colors
8. Erase past material

PRINCIPLES OF PRESENTATION:

1. Be considerate of entire audience
   - Do not allow anyone to dominate
   - Give answers understandable to everyone
   - Speak to all audience members
   - React to all questions or comments
2. Respond encouragingly
3. Be honest
4. Avoid confrontations (usually)

WHEN ANSWERING AUDIENCE QUESTIONS, DO TWO THINGS:

1. Analyze the question
   A. What is the intent of the question?
   B. What are the potential effects of answering?

2. Respond fully and carefully
   A. Repeat the question
   B. Rephrase if necessary
   C. Postpone troublesome questions
   D. Label and rephrase loaded questions
      — Be sure audience recognizes nature of question
      — Analyze the question
      — Use judgment in answering

Index